ENGLISH HERITAGE

Book of
York

D1358722

Genio Loci Feliciter

In appreciation of my precursors,
with thanks to helpful contemporaries and
as a drogue for them and for my post-cursers

ENGLISH HERITAGE

Book of York

Richard Hall

Richard Hall

B. T. Batsford / English Heritage
London

© Richard Hall 1996

First published 1996

All rights reserved. No part of this publication
may be reproduced in any form or by any means,
without permission from the Publisher

Typeset by Bernard Cavender Design & Greenwood Graphics Publishing
Printed and bound in Great Britain by
The Bath Press, Bath

Published by B.T. Batsford Ltd
4 Fitzhardinge Street, London W1H 0AH

A CIP catalogue record for this book is
available from the British Library

ISBN 0 7134 7719 9 (cased)
0 7134 7720 2 (limp)

Contents

Illustrations

Colour plates

Acknowledgements

My knowledge of York is based on the work and writings of numerous scholars, and has been furthered through conversations and correspondence with many of them. In particular, in the writing of this book I am grateful for the advice and comments of Peter Addyman, Lawrence Butler, Chris Daniell, Barrie Dobson, Rhona Finlayson, Tim Schadla-Hall, Sarah Jennings, Gillian Fellows Jensen, Jane Lilley, Ailsa Mainman, Jason Monaghan, Richard Morris, Patrick Ottaway, David Smith, Jim Spriggs, Ian Stead, Vivien Swan, Barbara Wilson and Ian Wood. None of those named above should be assumed necessarily to agree with what I have written.

I am also grateful to all my colleagues, past and present, at York Archaeological Trust. Individually and collectively, they have been responsible both for gathering the great majority of the data which is summarized here (often in less than wholly pleasant working conditions), and for studying and making sense of it. Their expertise and dedication to York have increased the understanding of the city's past enormously, although, as they would be the first to admit, there is still great potential for further work. Mention must also be made of English Heritage, who until now have funded most of the excavation and research carried out in York. Various developers and individuals have also made generous financial contributions towards excavation and research, with General Accident in particular having facilitated much archaeological research.

The illustrations have been generously provided by the York City Library branch of North Yorkshire County Library, where I am especially grateful to Gordon Hand and Amanda Howard (**10, 11**); York Minster Library, through the good offices of Sara Costley, Derek Phillips and Brenda Heywood and with the kind permission of the Dean and Chapter (**24, 25, 26, 27, 68, 83**); the National Monuments Record of the Royal Commission on the Historical Monuments of England, where Chris Chandler has dealt most efficiently with my requests (**2, 14, 86, 92, colour plate 6**); English Heritage, where Chris Evans has again been most helpful (**33, 34, 35, 69**); York City Archives and the city archivist, Rita Freedman (**29, 30**); York City Art Gallery and its curator Richard Green (**colour plate 12**); The British Library (**3**); The Company of Merchant Adventurers of the City of York, through the good offices of its Clerk, Ivison Wheatley (**72**); The Yorkshire Museum and its Keeper of Antiquities, Elizabeth Hartley and its Registrar, Melanie Baldwin (**19, 42, 77, 82, 90**); Dr Robin Birley and The Vindolanda Trust (**1**); Russell Wright of Wright Associates (**51**). The institutions named here retain the copyright on their illustrations. The cover picture and illustrations **7, 18, 20, 23, 28, 32, 38, 39, 47, 52, 62, 72, 73, 74, 75, 89** and **98** and **colour plates 10** and **11** are photographs by Simon I. Hill FRPS (Scirebröc) and, unless otherwise stated, are copyright of York Archaeological Trust. Illustration **31** and **colour plates 9, 14, 15** and **16** are the author's.

Other illustrations come from York Archaeological Trust. The drawings from York Archaeological Trust include the work of Charlotte Bentley (**41**), Kate Biggs (**6, 13, 15, 40, 65, 79**), Glenys Boyles (**3, 55, 81**), Cathy Brooks (**76**), Simon Chew (**colour plate 1**), Terry Finnemore (59), Sheena Howarth (**71, 96, 99**), Helen Humphreys (**91**), Peter Marshall (**94**) and Anne Thomas (**97**). Photographs from York Archaeological Trust were taken by John Bailey, Keith Buck, Tessa Bunney, Jan Dennis, Mike Duffy, Simon I. Hill and Arthur MacGregor, and made available through York Archaeological Trust Picture Library. York Archaeological Trust retains copyright of these illustrations. Peter Addyman, Glenys Boyles, Hilary Cool, Simon I. Hill, John Hutchinson, Christine Kyriacou, Peter Marshall, Hugh Murray, David Patrick and Stefan Sadowski at Impressions Gallery have also kindly helped in matters concerning the illustrations.

The manuscript has been nurtured by Sheila Cosgrove and Heather Dawson, and the whole work has benefited from comments by Ailsa Mainman, Patrick Ottaway and David Palliser. Peter Kemmis Betty and Charlotte Vickerstaff at Batsford have also kept helpful eyes on the project, and I am particularly grateful for their assistance in the latter stages.

To everyone mentioned above I extend my warmest thanks.

Any remaining errors of fact or peculiarities of interpretation are the sole responsibility of the author.

Preface

Writing books on York is a growth industry; it's an attractive and fascinating place to live in or to visit, and thus a good topic for publishers. Small enough to be 'manageable', its buildings are mostly on a human scale, varied in date and form, and not overwhelming. Its famed set pieces – the Minster, the walls, the castle – are supplemented by a wealth of medieval, post-medieval and modern churches, houses, alms-houses, guildhalls and commercial premises, and leavened by the ruins of monasteries, hospitals and earlier defences. For York has not suffered the extensive wartime damage of London or Southampton, and not seen the dreadful thoughtless developments which have defaced Worcester or Kings Lynn; it is largely intact in its form as a medieval city, and the legacy of earlier epochs can also be recognized. They bear witness to an importance as the political, social and, at times, even the economic 'capital of the North' over many centuries, and recorded history provides an outline of great events which goes back to the dawn of our era.

Not much was erected in the way of modern buildings during the nineteenth and early to mid-twentieth centuries, so little was laid as foundations to damage the layers of soil, debris and buried remains which form the main record for much of York's early existence and development. Archaeologists excavating in the city are therefore fortunate to work with what can be described as the most complete, if complex, archaeological deposits from an English city of long-lived and first-rank importance. And this is the rationale for 'another book about York', for I have chosen to concentrate on the penetrating new light which archaeology has shed upon what previously seemed some rather well-known aspects of life in York. I hope to demonstrate that York has been through many different guises and served many different purposes over the generations, and that its people have lived and worked through changing circumstances; that while some aspects of their lifestyles seem strange and outdated, others are recognizable and familiar. As any excavating archaeologist would, I hope to add a bit of depth and perspective to the view of York for both resident and visitor.

1
Discovering York

York has been written about almost since its foundation, nearly 2000 years ago. Many of the references – particularly those dating from before the Norman Conquest – are brief. A good example is the earliest: simply the Roman's name for York on the address side of a stylus tablet dated *c.* 95–104, found at the fort of Vindolanda, near Hadrian's Wall (**1**). In one sense this ephemeral reference contrasts starkly with Roman monumental stone inscriptions erected to commemorate building projects in the city (**2**), but both, in their different ways, are indications of Roman York's importance. Equally telling are the references by several

1 *The first record of York's existence – the Latin name-form EBURACI is part of the address on the outside of a wooden stylus tablet found at Vindolanda, Northumberland, and dated AD 97–102/3. Length: 0.145m (5¾in).*

2 *Reconstructed inscription from King's Square, recording a gateway erected by the Ninth Legion in AD 107–8. Height: 1.14m (3ft 9in).*

3 *Enhanced version of a general view of York in a c. 1320 manuscript of Geoffrey of Monmouth's* History of the Kings of Britain. *The Minster is at centre; ? St Mary's Abbey to the left. Royal Ms 13A III f16v* (By permission of the British Library).

Roman historians, which place York on a broader canvas.

Following Roman military withdrawal *c.* 400, written records are virtually absent for the fifth and sixth centuries, but the reintroduction of Christianity returned York to a literate ambit in the seventh century. Particularly important sources include Bede's *Ecclesiastical History of the English People*, written in *c.* 730, and the almost contemporary *Life of St Wilfrid*. Both provide information on political and religious events in the seventh century. The first general description and historical summary of York was given by the York cleric Alcuin in his poem *The Bishops, Kings and Saints of York*, composed *c.* 780–90. His picture of York, in an ideal landscape of flowering fields, on a river teeming with fish, founded by the Romans, who built high walls and lofty towers, is probably a mixture of literary convention, observation and extrapolation from towns on the Continent that he saw on his travels. For the Viking Age (866–1069) the most important single source is the *Anglo-Saxon Chronicle*, which provides at least intermittent references to political events in York, but with only incidental descriptive detail.

In these Anglian and Anglo-Scandinavian periods, and particularly in the tenth and eleventh centuries, the city's inhabitants certainly encountered remains of earlier epochs. Chance must have played its part. The digging of rubbish pits and other disturbances to the ground brought small but interesting items to the surface, for archaeologists find Roman coins, pottery sherds, glass fragments and many other objects in layers of much later date. For example, a coin of the Roman empress Julia Domna, dated *c.* 200, was found in a fifth-/sixth-century Anglo-Saxon pot at The Mount cremation cemetery. Sometimes, however, as with Roman building stone, later inhabitants were deliberately seeking earlier materials for reuse. What, if anything, the average townsfolk thought about the origins of these unfamiliar remains is largely unknowable. To eighth-century churchmen, however, such ancient items could be classified as the work of pagans; the service books of Egbert, Archbishop of York 735–66, contained a dedication used for purifying items dug out of the ground in order to make them suitable for Christian use.

William the Conqueror's 'Domesday Book' preserves a rather more factual and fiscal view of the city in 1086, and heralds an increasing range and diversity of sources from the twelfth century onwards. Their survival is a testimony to the care with which both secular and ecclesiastical authorities looked after their archives. Information also comes from a number of general histories which, naturally, incorporated events at York. Some of them also looked back to much earlier periods, and were prepared to invent when they had no certain information. Thus Geoffrey of Monmouth, in his *History of the Kings of Britain* written in 1135, invented a pre-Roman king, Ebrauk, as the city's founder. Life followed art; an image of Ebrauk was erected on the corner of Colliergate and Saviourgate. It was moved to the Guildhall Chapel in 1501 and in 1738 it was set in a niche on Bootham Bar, but by 1896 even its original shape, never mind any detail, was unrecognizable, and it was removed.

As the Middle Ages progressed, increasing numbers of visitors to York, both English and foreign, wrote down their impressions of the place. The earliest illustration to survive is a view of *c.* 1320 in which the most prominent buildings are churches (**3**); it mirrors the majority of written descriptions which, unsurprisingly, picked out the Minster for mention. Other obvious topics were the city walls and the castle. From the sixteenth century, however, when the famous antiquaries John Leland (*c.* 1506–52) and William Camden (1551–1623) visited and wrote lengthier accounts, there is a wider range of descriptions.

From about the same time it is possible to follow the city's development on a succession of maps and plans. Starting with a mid-sixteenth-century schematic plan on parchment (**4**), these continued via the measured plan of John Speed (1610) which incorporates three-dimensional views of contemporary buildings (**5**) to more standard eighteenth-century and later plans, and culminated in 1852 in the first edition Ordnance Survey map of York. These early plans sometimes show the ground plans of individual buildings in varying degrees of schematic form; luckily, from the seventeenth century onwards, artists drew and painted views and elevations of quite a considerable number of medieval and post-medieval buildings, structures, streetscapes and vistas which have subsequently disappeared (**colour plate 12**).

In tandem with the capture of old, romantic York by artists there was an increasing interest in the history of York. After Roger Dodsworth (1585–1654) collected information about church monuments in the city *c.* 1620, the next notable figure was Sir Thomas Widdrington (*c.* 1600–64). As Recorder of York, he was in a good position to compile the first narrative history of the city; however, it was not published until the nineteenth century, and so other, rather later historians are better known. Among them the eccentric York printer Thomas Gent (1693–1778) deserves mention for his *History of the Famous City of York* (1730). Pride of place, however, for its accuracy and range, goes to *Eboracum*, published in 1736 by the city surgeon Francis Drake (1696–1771), who was both a Fellow of the Royal Society and a Fellow of the Society of Antiquaries. This tradition of local interest, not unusually, was maintained and enhanced through the later eighteenth and nineteenth centuries.

Yet another strand in the historical process was the recovery of ancient remains, both buildings and objects, which lay buried beneath the city. The intrinsic interest of such discoveries was recognized as early as 1579 when a stone coffin, inscribed with a Latin text, was found *c.* 400m (¼ mile) west of the city walls. It had belonged to Verecundius Diogenes, a leading Roman citizen of York, and was noted by William Camden in his *Britannia*. Later it was taken to Hull, and was last seen there in the eighteenth century, acting as a horse trough at the Coach and Horses Inn.

Other pieces of decorated Roman stonework, including altars and tombstones, were collected in the seventeenth century, and some of them survive to the present day. Large, elaborate, almost indestructible, and carrying Latin texts which any well-educated person could translate, their interest was obvious. Smaller or fragmentary items must have been seen when earthmoving took place, but were, apparently, generally ignored. Exceptions, however, included coin hoards, like that dating from the reign of William the Conqueror found in High Ousegate (**6**) in 1696 when a burned-down house was being replaced.

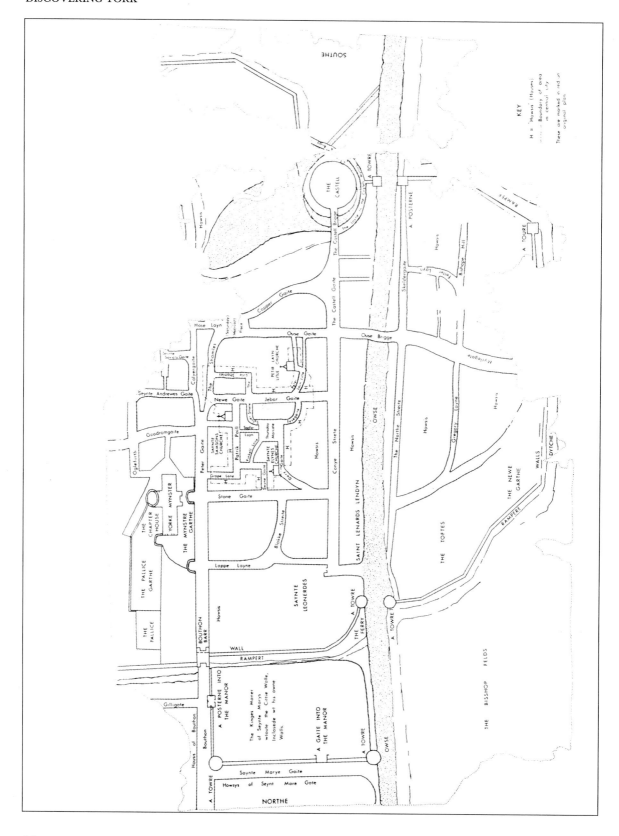

4 Schematic plan of York c. 1545; drawn from an original, on two damaged sheets of parchment, in the Public Record Office (MPB 49,51).

Once ancient coins had become collectable, other everyday items were also sought after. The Georgian and Victorian periods provided golden opportunities – house-building in the city and the suburbs combined with industrial developments such as the railway stations – to disturb large areas with notable buried remains.

Even some of the most obvious and illustrious remnants of antiquity were threatened by

redevelopment proposals. In 1800 York Corporation petitioned Parliament for permission to remove the bars, walls and posterns of York, on the grounds that they were inconvenient for access, decayed and costly to repair. A preservation lobby was formed with both local and national supporters including Sir Walter Scott, and Parliament, perhaps remembering that York had been refortified as recently as the Jacobite uprising of 1745, rejected the idea on the grounds of defence of the realm. The Corporation backed

5 John Speed's plan of York, engraved in 1610.

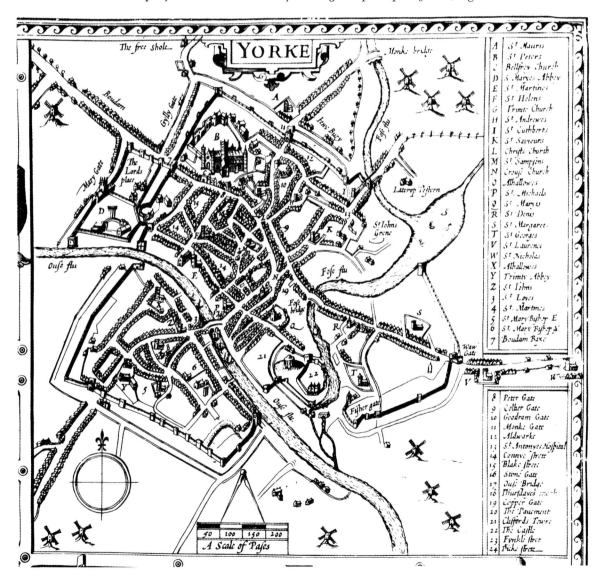

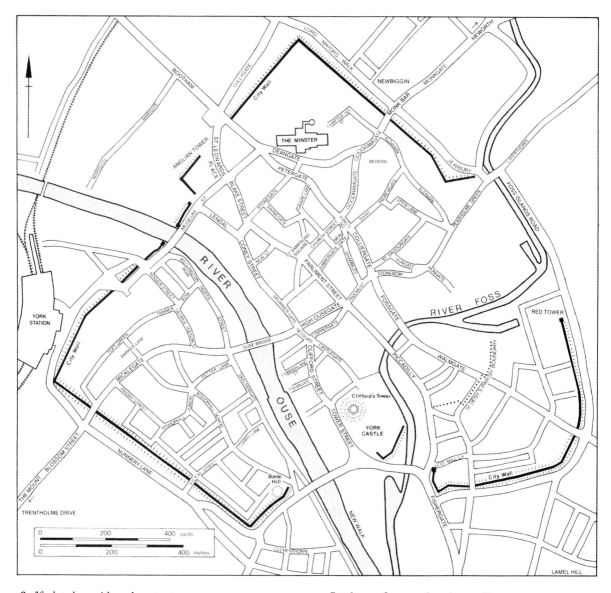

6 *York today, with modern street names.*

off, and most of the walls were saved for the time being. In the following decades, however, various demolitions took place, so that in 1827 the York Footpath Association, under the chairmanship of the Archbishop of York, proposed that the walls should be restored, through public subscription, to their pristine state. Among the fundraising ploys was a County Ball, given at York in 1834 under the patronage of the Lord Mayor and Lady Mayoress, which prompted the following verse:

In days of yore, the city walls,
Were battered and laid waste by *balls*
But Lady Mayoress, through your care,
A *Ball* will now the walls repair.

Some restoration was indeed undertaken, but the Corporation also continued with its attrition of the fabric through demolition and desecration. In 1839 the York artist William Etty spoke out again for complete restoration, suggesting that the walls were a tourist attraction. He wrote: 'Beware how you destroy your antiquities, guard them with religious care. They are what give you a decided character and superiority over other provincial cities. You have lost much – take care of what remains!'

It was the controversies of the earlier nineteenth century which raised public awareness and appreciation of the city walls and other ancient structures as monuments of historic importance. Yet still there were proposals for destruction. Perhaps the most barmy (in retrospect) was that of 1855 when the Board of Health Committee proposed to remove the walls between the Red Tower and Walmgate Bar on the grounds that they harmed local residents by preventing a free circulation of air. Fortunately, the idea failed to gain support. Although wholesale destruction was again an issue as late as 1905, the Lord Mayor of 1904 was swimming with the public tide when he said, 'the Corporation is now fully alive to the necessity of not only sparing, but also of preserving all those remains of the past which either from their antiquity or beauty are left to us, and are amongst our most cherished possessions.'

Appreciation of buried monuments and remains was also growing. Already, in 1822, polite society in the city and county had formed the Yorkshire Philosophical Society to further the study of geology and archaeology, and acquired the area occupied by the ruins of St Mary's Abbey in which to erect a museum and lay out gardens and grounds. From 1827, they sponsored what might be described as the first archaeological excavation in York, albeit amounting to no more than the clearance of rubble and debris from the Abbey's ruins (7). There was another kind of clearance after a fire in York Minster in 1829 destroyed the choir; the scheme for rebuilding required excavation, which was undertaken and recorded by the local artist and antiquary John Browne (1793–1877). It revealed part of a Norman crypt, which had been infilled in the fourteenth–fifteenth centuries, as well as other traces of early buildings.

The pace of development, and antiquaries seizing their opportunities, brought to light so many new discoveries that by 1842 Revd

7 *Nash's engraving of clearance work at St Mary's Abbey chapter-house* c. *1827.*

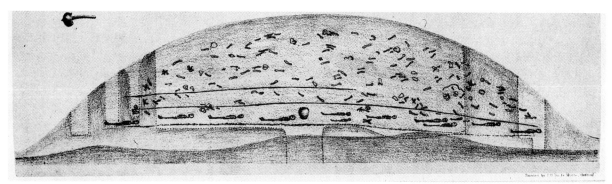

8 *Lamel Hill; Thurnam's 1848 cross-section showing the cemetery and disturbed bones in the later, Civil War-period mound above.*

Charles Wellbeloved (1769–1858) could publish a work exploring just a single period. His *Eboracum: York Under the Romans* incorporated drawings and descriptions of the Roman defensive walls, stone buildings, inscribed coffins and altars, pottery, tiles, coins, and decorated metalwork. In 1846 a further boost was given to matters archaeological and antiquarian when the [Royal] Archaeological Institute of Great Britain and Ireland held what was only its second Annual Summer Meeting in York – a meeting largely underwritten by George Hudson, the city's 'Railway King'.

Another index of an increasingly methodical approach was shown in 1864 when Robert Skaife (1830–1916) published a *Plan of Roman, Medieval and Modern York*. Shortly thereafter the Archbishop of York became President of an archaeological charity – but, in keeping with the times, it was the Palestine Exploration Fund rather than something on his doorstep. Nonetheless, a succession of *Handbooks to the Collections of the Yorkshire Philosophical Society*, which went through eight editions between 1852 and 1891, record not only a growing archaeological collection from the city but one which was increasingly understood and correctly dated.

The first recognizable archaeological excavation in York took place in 1847–8, inspired and directed by John Thurnam (1810–73), Medical Superintendent of The Retreat, England's first mental hospital. In the grounds of The Retreat

was a large mound, Lamel Hill; landscaping *c.* 1840 brought human bones to the surface.

'[Thurnam] was sufficiently interested by the results already obtained to make arrangements, in which a few friends united, for a more systematic investigation of this place of burial . . . After digging several deep holes in various directions in the sides of the tumulus . . . a horizontal shaft, about four feet wide, and six and a half feet high, was commenced . . . After tunnelling in the way described, for about forty feet, almost to the centre of the mound, further progress was impeded by the falling in from the surface of a considerable portion of the superincumbent soil.' (*Archaeological Journal*, 1849)

Unharmed and undeterred by this potentially fatal accident, Thurnam and his collaborators returned to trenching down from the surface, and explored a large part of the buried ground surface. Below the centre of the mound they revealed what he took to be a Roman cremation urn (now thought to date from the seventeenth-century Civil War activity here); all around were human skeletons, laid out regularly on an east-west alignment. By a process of eliminating other options Thurnam came to the tentative conclusion that they were of Anglo-Saxon date.

In many ways, Thurnam's investigation was remarkably advanced for its time. He produced a drawing of the layers and features seen in the side of this trench, still a standard archaeological practice today (**8**); he paid detailed attention not only to associated objects but to animal bones; the human skeletal remains were identified and measured with considerable care; with the aid of a microscope he identified the species represented in wood residues adhering to iron coffin fittings and in deposits of charcoal; he undertook chemical analyses of some deposits; and he used a x250 microscope to view organic residues within the supposed Roman urn. Beyond this, he ranged widely through English and European parallels for his discoveries, and called upon classical and later written sources to support his arguments. Truly a remarkable and precocious archaeological performance. What else might he have done if providence hadn't taken him from York?

Thurnam's interest in human skeletal remains and skull measurements was revived when earthmoving for the building of the present railway station in 1870–3 uncovered part of a Roman cemetery. The remains were sent to the first professor of physiology at Oxford University; they were restudied in 1935 for a report on 'The Racial Affinities of the Romano-British'.

The early decades of the twentieth century, a time when the North Eastern Railway was already featuring 'Historic York' in its advertizing, saw more frequent attempts to study the city's buried remains. The York architect George Benson (1856–1935) undertook what today would be termed 'watching briefs' – that is, simply visiting building sites to record what the labourers had uncovered during their work. Benson salvaged what information he could from sites in High Ousegate, Castlegate and at York Castle, where he took advantage of underpinning works and recorded the various layers which make up the Norman mound (**9**), including, apparently, two sets of timber remains, perhaps representing wooden towers. Meanwhile another, more celebrated, York architect, Walter Brierley (1862–1926), had continued with the clearance of St Mary's Abbey, and in consultation with the eminent antiquarian W. St John Hope devised a means of displaying the

9 *George Benson's 1902 reconstructed cross-section through the Norman castle motte and Clifford's Tower at York Castle.*

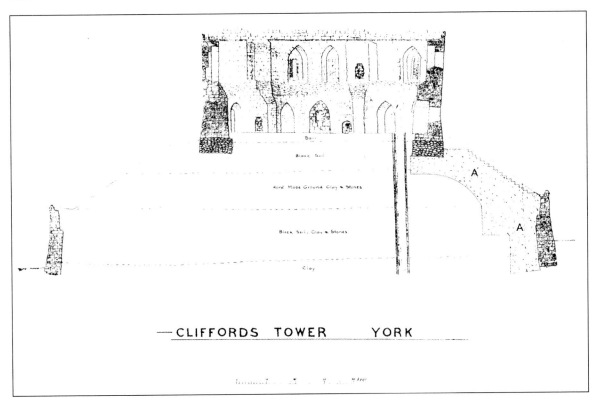

—CLIFFORDS TOWER YORK

10 *Miller's 1925 excavations at the east angle of the Roman fortress.*

discoveries, distinguishing different periods with different coloured brickwork. This gave rise to 'much comment and criticism on the part of many who do not clearly understand the real nature of the case, and the difficulties to be contended with'; a type of debate still familiar.

Archaeological excavations planned and executed to answer research questions started in York in 1925, under the auspices of the York Roman Excavations Committee. Steuart Napier Miller (1880–1952) excavated at several places along the line of the Roman fortress defences, single-mindedly pursuing remains of the Roman era. Important discoveries were made and promptly published; and already archaeology in York was a spectator sport (**10**). Yet, when the work ended after four short seasons, it was not followed up with more research-oriented archaeological excavations.

Shortly afterwards, however, extensive remains of a large Roman bath-house were revealed within the Roman fortress as new cellars were dug out by workmen below the Mail Coach Inn at St Sampson's Square (**11**). A local historian, Revd Angelo Raine, undertook some limited archaeological investigation, and the site was analysed and published by Philip Corder (1891–1961), a master at Bootham School in York who subsequently became a professional archaeologist. The main outcome of the discovery, and a foretaste of things to come, was that John Smith's Tadcaster Brewery Ltd altered their plans and enlarged the cellar, so that as much as possible of the baths could be revealed and preserved. They remain visible to this day.

York escaped World War II almost unscathed, and so there were not the tragic opportunities for archaeology among the ruins that occurred, for example, in London or Canterbury. Furthermore, the pulling-power of the city's heritage showed itself when, in 1948, the Council for British

Archaeology held its first summer conference in York. There were, however, requirements for new buildings in the late 1940s, and one of these schemes, for a telephone exchange by the banks of the River Foss in Hungate, was notable for spawning the first archaeological excavation in York which uncovered and recorded substantial Viking Age features. Kathleen Richardson, a protegée of Sir Mortimer Wheeler, brought to light what she interpreted as a Viking Age river embankment, together with an array of associated objects; their publication was a timely reminder of the unusual information which lay buried in York.

The 1950s and 1960s brought first a trickle and then a stream of redevelopment proposals. Even as late as 1966 some very important sites were developed without any form of archaeological record but with the inevitable destruction of buried remains. Increasingly, however, some small-scale archaeological observation or excavation was permitted by site owners (at least one of whom belonged to a short-lived York Excavation Committee), and usually paid for by the Ministry of Public Buildings and Works, the forerunner of English Heritage. The directors of these rescue excavations were sometimes imported from outside the city, but more often they were local experts. Herman Ramm (1922–91), employed in the newly created York office of the Royal Commission on the Historical Monuments of England, Peter Wenham (1911–90), Head of the Department of History at St John's Teacher Training College, York, and his protegé Ian Stead, a York-born Cambridge archaeology undergraduate destined for the British Museum, all directed fairly small-scale excavations, mainly along the Roman fortress defences or aimed at other Roman targets. Their efforts provided a sound basis of information which was taken a stage further by Jeffrey Radley (1935–70), also from the York office of the Royal Commission on the Historical Monuments of England, who seized the opportunities for observation and recording which a quickening pace of redevelopment was presenting. Tragically, in 1970, while investigating the city's pre-Norman defences,

Radley was killed when the side of his trench collapsed.

One other major archaeological project of this era was the investigation below and around York Minster during 1966–73. It was initiated as a subterfuge to allow an appraisal of the state of the cathedral's foundations; as the necessary remedial civil engineering progressed, excavation continued in extremely difficult conditions, directed by Derek Phillips. It showed that the Anglo-Saxon and Viking Age cathedral does not lie below its Norman and medieval successor, although parts of a Viking Age graveyard were recovered.

In 1972 archaeology in York entered a new era when the local awareness of the Yorkshire Philosophical Society and the national perspective of the Council for British Archaeology converged. Their mutual concern was the amount of archaeological disturbance likely to result from proposals both to create an inner ring road and to undertake other large-scale rebuilding. Their answer was the establishment of a professional archaeological unit, York Archaeological Trust for Excavation and Research (YAT), under the direction of Peter Addyman. Throughout the 1970s and early 1980s the Ancient Monuments Inspectorate of the Ministry of Public Buildings and Works, and its successors, paid YAT to undertake a series of excavations and to research

11 *A faded but precious record of the 1930 discovery of a Roman bath-house at St Sampson's Square.*

12 *Just ahead of the redevelopment contractors, hurried excavation and recording of well-preserved Viking Age–Norman timber features at the Queen's Hotel, 1–9 Micklegate in 1988.*

and publish the data thus recovered. The facilities created to assist in this process included an archaeological conservation laboratory, latterly incorporating the York Archaeological Wood Centre, a nationally recognized focus of excellence, and a pioneering Environmental Archaeological Unit, subsequently relocated at the University of York. A measure of the success which YAT has achieved can be seen in its internationally renowned Jorvik Viking Centre and its Archaeological Resource Centre; it has also published nearly 50 books in its series of reports *The Archaeology of York*.

By the mid 1980s, however, moves were afoot to change the basis on which excavations were funded, with the Government wishing to apply the 'polluter pays' principle to archaeology. In York this coincided with a *cause célèbre* when the City Council, eager to bring new employers to the city, watched in horror as the National Curriculum Council's relocation to new offices in Micklegate was threatened by public outcry over the potential destruction of archaeological remains which had been ignored in the negotiations. Everybody involved – central government, local government, the NCC and the developer – thought someone else should pay for the archaeological investigation. No one wanted to alter the building's design fundamentally, for example by removing the requirement for a basement; all were united in the concern that excavation would delay building work to an unacceptable extent. Eventually a compromise was worked out, which kept the NCC in York and allowed a minimal amount of excavation (**12**).

This case, and others in London, were in the forefront of ensuring a change in procedures. In 1990 central government guidance to local government planners effectively passed the responsibility for funding excavations to the developers whose new structures were destroying the archaeology. York City Council, with English Heritage backing, appointed an archaeologist to its Planning Department, and it is he who now determines what archaeological work should take place before any redevelopment scheme goes ahead. Specifications for these works are now put out to competitive tender to various archaeological organizations, and developers appoint the archaeological contractor which offers the lowest price – wide-ranging background understanding of a particular locale, patiently accumulated through many years of study, and a special knowledge of its archaeology, both of which allow a deeper comprehension of new discoveries, carry no premium. The result of all these changes has been that developers are much more willing to minimize the amount of archaeological damage they inflict through basements or foundations, and in consequence there is much less archaeological excavation in York than a decade ago. At this period of hiatus the time is ripe, therefore, to summarize the current state of knowledge.

2

A place in time

Historic Yorkshire, that part of north-east England bounded by the Humber Estuary, the River Tees and the Pennine Hills, is split up the middle from north to south by a relatively low-lying belt of land which was fashioned by glaciers during the last Ice Age. It includes the narrow, irregular Vale of Mowbray in its northern part and the wider Vale of York in the south. Together they form the easiest natural north-south route-way through the area, for to the east rise the Yorkshire Moors and Yorkshire Wolds, while on the west flank are the foothills of the Yorkshire Dales. When the glacier's front was static, its rate of advance balanced by its rate of melt, the boulder clay, sands, gravels and other geological debris transported in the ice were deposited at its melting edge. When the glacier finally retreated, this debris remained and formed a well-drained ridge, called a moraine, which made a natural east-west routeway, about 1.6km (a mile) wide and 1.5–7.5m (5–25 ft) high, right across the lower lying Vale (**13**).

The region's river systems naturally flowed into the Vale, the largest valley in northern England, and the main river, the Ouse, cut its way through the moraine. It broke through midway across the 40km- (25-mile) wide Vale, at a point where it was joined by its tributary, the River Foss. The angle of land above their junction, on the north-east bank of the Ouse, was relatively flat, dipping sharply only at the lips of the two river valleys. On the opposite bank of the Ouse, in contrast, there was a marked upslope, in two principal steps.

The River Ouse flows into the Humber Estuary, and was naturally tidal up to and indeed beyond the point where it breached the moraine. Thus the countryside up to the moraine ridge could easily be reached by ship-borne traffic, which was assisted by the tidal motion. It was 60km (38 miles) from the moraine to the mouth of the Ouse, and the same distance along the estuary to the open sea.

There is archaeological evidence that prehistoric peoples passed along the natural routeways that converge here and settled, either temporarily or permanently, in the vicinity (**14**). From the eighth/seventh millennium BC Mesolithic communities were in the region, which must have had attractions for hunters and fishermen. The farmers of the Neolithic Period (*c.* 4000–*c.* 2000 BC) utilized the moraine – their presence is indicated by characteristic polished stone axes which have been found at several sites, with a particularly notable concentration by the Ouse, on the south-west bank. Activity or occupation continued in the vicinity during the Bronze Age (*c.* 2000–*c.* 700 BC); for example, a hoard of flint tools and weapons, possibly dating to the early Bronze Age, was found in 1868 during building of the North Eastern Railway Gasworks near the junction of Holgate Beck with the River Ouse, and a 'Beaker' pottery vessel, perhaps from a burial, was found in Bootham in 1840.

By the end of the Iron Age in the first century AD, and perhaps for some centuries before, the area seems to have been in the boundary zone

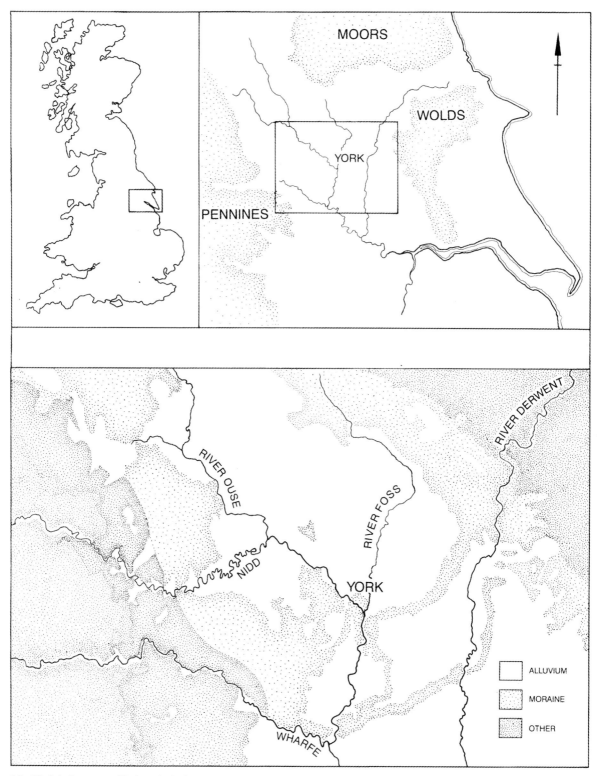

13 *York in its geographical, geological and topographical setting.*

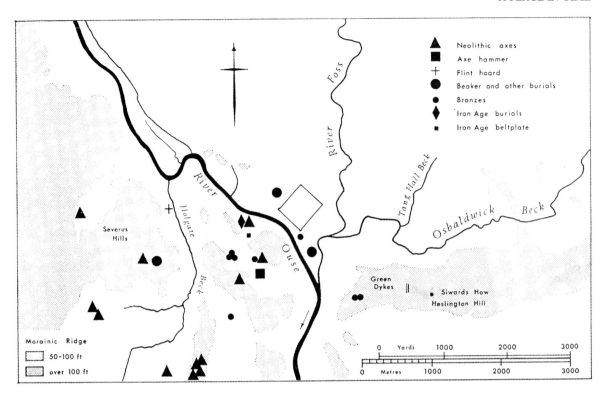

14 *Prehistoric finds in the vicinity of York.*

between the Brigantes, a large and powerful tribal confederacy which controlled much of northern England, and the Parisi, who occupied the Wolds area of eastern Yorkshire. Until quite recently it was believed that these people made little use of the low-lying Vale of York because they preferred the better-drained upland soils, but new discoveries are now requiring a revision of this view. Some 4.7km (3 miles) south-east of York at Lingcroft Farm, Dr Rick Jones of Bradford University has uncovered traces of a late Iron Age farmstead, and in 1993 YAT explored an extensive Iron Age settlement near Easingwold, 24km (15 miles) north-west of the city.

There is surprisingly little evidence for the Iron Age in the immediate vicinity of York itself; the nearest occurrence of Iron Age pottery comes from Rawcliffe, 4km (2¼ miles) to the north-west. The city's Roman name, *Eboracum*, is derived from a British Celtic name meaning either 'the place of the yew trees' or 'the field of Eburos', but if there was a Celtic landowner

named Eburos living hereabouts in the pre-Roman period, there is as yet no trace of his field ditches, let alone his farmstead.

In AD 71 native self-determination came to an end when the Romans took over the area. Previously the north-eastern frontier of their province of *Britannia* had been the Humber, with military control exercised from Lincoln. They had treated the Brigantes as 'clients', probably both bribing and threatening them into forming a peaceful buffer zone beyond the Humber. But when Brigantian politics made confrontation imminent and inevitable, the Romans struck northwards. The Ninth Legion advanced and built a fortress to dominate the newly annexed area.

The military surveyors recognized the distinct advantages which the site of York offered, and this military judgment has had lasting influence on the city (**15**). The relatively flat area in the wedge of land between the two rivers provided a site big enough to contain a standard-sized 20-hectare (50-acre) legionary fortress, and in varying degrees the Roman defences and internal layout constrained and affected how the site

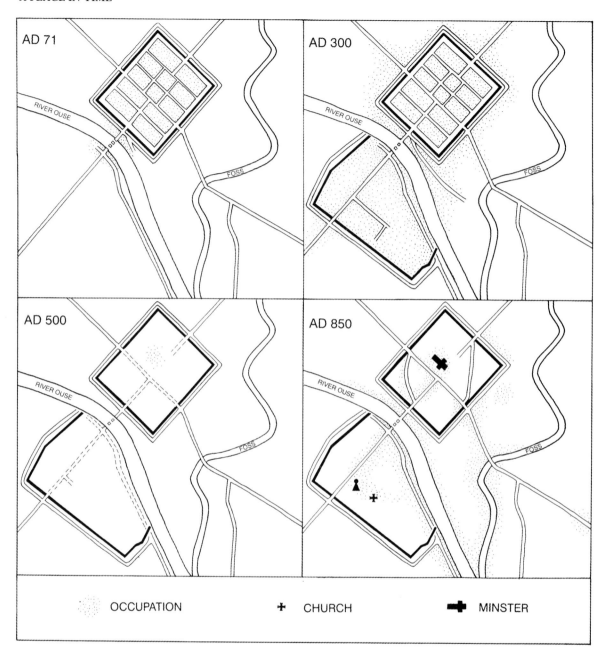

15 *York's development through the ages.*

would be used in future centuries. The rivers provided extra protective barriers beyond the south-east and south-west sides of the fortress, and both could give berths for vessels bringing military supplies to the fortress – supplies which might come not just from the garrison's hinterland, or even elsewhere in the province, but direct from the Continent if needs be. With secure supply lines, attention could be focused on controlling movements up and down the corridor of the Vale of York, and using the natural causeway of the moraine to move troops speedily either eastwards towards the Parisi or westwards into Brigantian territory.

When *Eboracum* was founded the Roman empire was still expanding, and there was no guarantee

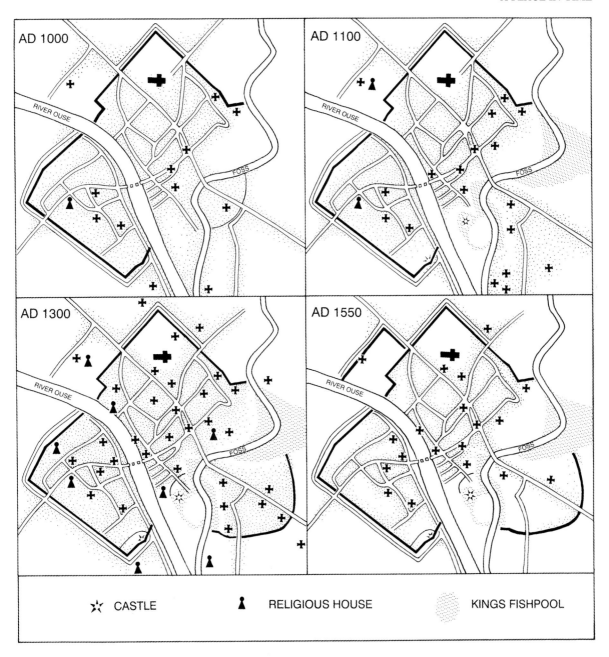

AD 1000

AD 1100

AD 1300

AD 1550

☆ CASTLE　　　　　♦ RELIGIOUS HOUSE　　　　　KINGS FISHPOOL

that York would remain a permanent fortress; indeed, Roman historians relate that various commanders pushed further northwards in the following decades. So although the timber buildings within the fortress required renovation or reconstruction within 20–30 years, much of the fortress continued to be built of relatively impermanent materials. By 107–8 at least one of the gateways was rebuilt in stone, strengthening a

potential weak point and providing an opportunity for a stonecarver to create a most elegant inscription which tells us the date (see **2**). Inside the fortress, the only buildings which are known to have been built of stone at this time are the bathhouse and the headquarters building (*principia*).

Yet even then the long-term future of *Eboracum* may still have been in doubt. Excavations at 9 Blake Street (currently the Stonegate Arcade)

16 *A cross-section of Roman activity below 39 Coney Street; at the bottom, the dark slots and floor of a beetle-infested storehouse, sealed below a clay dump on which a second storehouse was erected. Covered by fire debris, it was sealed by Roman road surfaces, truncated by the modern cellar floor. Scale: 1m (39in).*

revealed a distinct absence of pottery datable between *c.* 120 and *c.* 160; perhaps much of the garrison was based elsewhere, building Hadrian's Wall and then pressing further north to the Antonine Wall, between the Forth and the Clyde. Only when that defensive system was judged a wall too far, and Hadrian's Wall refortified, was a long-term future for *Eboracum* secured and the fortress renovated with stone walls and stone buildings throughout. Areas beyond the walls were also replanned – for example by the River Ouse, where timber warehouses erected in the early years of conquest were replaced by a new street system (**16**).

This new feeling of permanence probably encouraged civilians to develop the area on the south-west bank of the River Ouse, where a relatively level plateau was separated from a levelish shelf beside the river by a steep slope. This developed area grew rapidly in the late second century, and by 237 had been awarded official status as a *colonia*, the highest grade of civilian town. There were only four *coloniae* in the Roman province of *Britannia*, and the other three (Colchester, Gloucester and Lincoln) were all former fortresses which had been declared colonies for retired veterans. *Colonia Eboracensis* (**17**) stands out as a later creation where, so far as the limited evidence shows, politics and economics were the driving force behind its rapid development.

In contrast with other towns in *Britannia*, *Colonia Eboracensis* flourished in the third century, when London and other southern towns were economically stagnant or in decline. It must have been given a boost in 208–11 when the emperor Septimius Severus, his wife Julia Domna, and their son Caracalla used it as a base for campaigns to the north of Hadrian's Wall. Severus died in York, and Caracalla swiftly returned to Rome to secure the succession. By 216 he had split the province of Britain into two, and confirmed York as the capital of *Britannia Inferior* (Lower Britain). Many of the city's public buildings, commercial warehouses and villas for the well-to-do were probably constructed *c.* 200–50, and a defensive wall was erected (see **15**).

Under the emperor Diocletian, in the late third century, the two provinces of Britain were again subdivided, and *Eboracum* became the capital of *Britannia Secunda*. At about this time the Roman army in northern England was restructured under the command of the Duke of the Britains (*dux Britanniarum*); *Eboracum* was probably his base and residence.

The early fourth century saw another emperor and his son in residence; Constantius, like his predecessors, was campaigning to the north. Once again, there must have been a beneficial impact on the local economy and there may have been rebuilding to impress the emperor; the number of early fourth-century mosaics shows private wealth being deployed at about this time. Constantius died at *Eboracum* in 306, and Constantine was immediately hailed as successor. Constantine proclaimed the toleration of Christianity throughout the empire in 313; by 314 *Eboracum* was a bishopric.

By this time the Roman military machine was on a very different footing, both in terms of

17 *Fragmentary Roman sarcophagus from 46–54 Fishergate; the top line of the inscription includes* CO[L] EBOR, *short for* colonia Eboracensis; *a reference to a* colonia-*status town at York.*

manpower and deployment. As early as the third century there had apparently been changes within the fortress; for example, the bath complex was demolished, yet the south-west defences were aggrandized (**18**). From the early fourth century some internal streets were no longer swept clean, but began to accumulate a layer of silt. By the later fourth century more military buildings were being demolished, although others were occupied continuously up to 400 and perhaps beyond. Similarly, there are signs that the extra-mural area around the fortress was abandoned in the mid to late fourth century, while across the river Ouse, in the *colonia*, public buildings seem to have been neglected and in decay. Yet private houses, notably the suburban villas, continued to be occupied beyond 400.

The big difficulty is in dating these last vestiges of Roman occupation. By *c.* 400 the army had officially been withdrawn from *Britannia* – but who knows how effective discipline was by then? It is entirely possible that some soldiers could have disobeyed their orders and, after a period Absent Without Leave, returned to their long-time home in the fortress. Yet such deserters no longer received pay or rations, and would have had to become self-sufficient. With Roman coinage no longer entering Britain, archaeologists lose their most common, and therefore most useful, form of dating evidence. In the absence of dendrochronological datings, and with the imprecision of carbon-14 determinations, uncertainty about the validity of archaeomagnetic dates for this epoch, and a dearth of datable artefacts, even pottery, we enter a chronological wilderness.

Various efforts have been made to explain the obscurity of fifth- to sixth-century York. One view is that for some time it was in a no-man's-land between advancing Anglo-Saxon invaders and retreating but tenacious Britons, who had been pushed back into the kingdom of Elmet, centred to the west of York around Leeds. Another idea, perhaps bolstered by recent experience, has been that large, low-lying tracts of York were uninhabitable because a long-term rise in the water-level led to widespread flooding in the fifth and sixth centuries,

but no supporting evidence for such a flooding has been recognized in excavations in York.

Part of the problem is that very few sites have been excavated carefully enough to recover the evidence in sufficient detail to give confidence to its interpretation. As late as the mid-1960s the dull layers cloaking Roman buildings were almost always removed in some or other degree of haste, so that upstanding remains could be exposed. Even quite recently, pressures of time created by redevelopment schedules have often denied excavators the opportunity to probe the subtleties of these enigmatic layers.

Therefore, the immediately 'post-Roman' period remains elusive. It's not clear how long a sub-Roman lifestyle could have been continued in and around a gradually decaying *Eboracum*. Indeed, what functions could the place have served? Among the possible answers are a continuing role as a seat of some more regionalized, even localized, political power. There are no records of how the Britons in the Vale of York organized themselves after the Romans' departure, but comparison with some other areas within and just beyond *Britannia* suggests that small successor states emerged in the fifth century. The British pre-Roman tribal base had not been extinguished by three and a half centuries of Roman rule; the political vacuum will have encouraged, even required, new leaders. The argument goes that, as a symbol of the previous authority, occupation of *Eboracum* would have conferred an aura of respectability and continuity upon a newly emerged local native leader. Furthermore, even in decay, the walls would have been defensible in case of attack by rivals, while some of its Roman buildings, although perhaps in a patched-up or even a ramshackle state, would have provided a relatively imposing setting for ceremony and occupation.

So runs the theory. Because of the dearth of evidence noted previously, proving or disproving it is contentious. The difficulties are beautifully demonstrated by the various possible interpretations of the remarkable discoveries below York Minster. In tracing the development

18 *The Multangular Tower in Museum Gardens; the west corner tower of the Roman fortress with medieval renovation above.*

of the Roman military *principia*, the headquarters building at the centre of the fortress, and its immediate vicinity, a complicated sequence of structural changes and a series of unusual layers were uncovered. The sequence clearly represents considerable changes in use and in lifestyle hereabouts; the problem is to determine when these changes occurred. There are three possible scenarios. One is that they all belong to a brief but bountiful late Roman episode, and that the site was then deserted until the Viking Age. A second possibility is that late Roman activities were continued into a sub-Roman phase of occupation in the fifth century, but that the site was then abandoned until the ninth century. The third interpretation allows an extended timescale for these events, embracing the late

Roman, sub-Roman and Anglian periods. More research is clearly needed to resolve this uncertainty.

Whatever the truth about sub-Roman British leaders occupying York, the late fifth or sixth century saw a new and important element introduced to the region with the arrival of immigrants from Denmark, Germany and the Low Countries – the Anglo-Saxons. Their cemeteries, rather than their houses, signal their presence around York; groups of characteristically shaped and decorated cremation urns have been found both to the south-west and the north-east of the

Roman settlement, at The Mount and at Heworth, and other characteristically Anglo-Saxon objects have also been recovered (**19**, see **15**).

These places are about 500m (550yds) and 800m (875yds) respectively from the Roman walls, and it is not clear whether the cemeteries belonged to communities living inside or outside those walls. The Anglo-Saxons who migrated to England came from an area which had not been under Roman occupation, and which did not have any towns. They were essentially farmers, and customarily built their houses from timber and thatch. The stone-using technology of the Romans was foreign to them, and they could not have maintained the stone-built structures of Roman York except in a most rudimentary fashion. One stone monument, the Anglian Tower (**20**), was named in the belief that it belongs to this period; now, however, it is generally thought more likely to be very late Roman in date. Indeed, by the time of the Anglo-Saxon arrival the interiors of both fortress and *colonia* may have been strewn with rubble, and potentially dangerous from collapsing buildings. York may have been a place to avoid, and such factors may

20 *The 'Anglian Tower' behind the City Library off Museum Street, more likely to be a late Roman addition to the fortress defences.*

account for the paucity of everyday objects of sixth- and seventh-century types in the city.

Nonetheless, seventh-century York, which the Anglo-Saxons called *Eoforwic*, is more clearly visible in both historical and archaeological terms. Bede's *Ecclesiastical History of the English People* records that in 627 the Northumbrian King, Edwin, was converted to Christianity and baptized in York; the small wooden church which he built then was the direct forerunner of York Minster. Christianity was advertized by the appearance of a cross design on mid-seventh-century gold coins found, and probably struck, in York. The papal mission reintroduced aspects of Mediterranean culture into Northumbria, and this was accentuated when the Pope created a bishop of York, perhaps in 625, and then, in 735, an archbishop. Learning was also fostered in the monastery which was created in the eighth century – for a time, *Eoforwic* enjoyed a European reputation for scholarship. To locate and explore this monastery, which may well be in the vicinity of Holy Trinity Church, Micklegate, would be one of the most exciting archaeological projects in York.

Until the mid-1980s, however, there was an overriding riddle about *Eoforwic*: was there an Anglian settlement at York apart from the royal and religious enclaves: if so what did it consist of, and where was it? No seventh- to ninth-century houses, no warehouses or other secular structures had been recognized inside the walls of either the fortress or the *colonia*. And although this could be explained by the same reasons which account for the absence of sub-Roman discoveries, the fact that only a small number of seventh- to ninth-century objects had ever been recovered in those areas seemed to confirm that they were not intensively occupied. The archaeological data did not seem to add up to the debris of the thriving commercial city which could be inferred from the historical documents. Admittedly, some other

19 *Anglian cremation urn of late fifth-/sixth century date from Heworth. Height: 0.24m (9½ins)* (Reproduced by courtesy of the Yorkshire Museum).

historically important contemporary settlements, particularly London, had a similar worrying gap in their archaeological record, but this did not diminish the problem for York's archaeologists.

One clue to solving the difficulty appeared in excavations in 1985–6 at Fishergate, close to the confluence of the rivers Ouse and Foss (see **15**). Totally unexpectedly, traces of several eighth- to ninth-century buildings were uncovered (**21**), together with evidence for a series of crafts/industries, domestic occupation and commerce. Initially, it looked as if there was a new, separate focus of secular occupation at that time, sited outside the fortress. Since then, however, further discoveries, although often made in small-scale excavations, have refocused the picture. It now seems more likely that there was a long, linear settlement in the seventh–ninth centuries, running along the banks of the Ouse and part of the Foss. There may also, of course, have been other foci of settlement which have not yet been recognized at all. Yet, although we know rather little in detail about *Eoforwic*, it was obviously a unique place within the kingdom of Northumbria, with

21 *An eighth-/ninth-century Anglian building at Fishergate – an excavation assistant stands in each of the post-holes for a timber roof support. Other features include contemporary and later pits, and walls and foundation trenches for the later Gilbertine monastery.*

its blend of royal, religious and economic functions in and around large, fortified areas.

Although there are no references to Viking attacks on *Eoforwic* during the early–mid-ninth century, when they raided some coastal sites in the kingdom, the Vikings clearly recognized its importance, for it was the first target of the invading *'great army'*. The good natural lines of communication worked to the attackers' advantage (they came overland from East Anglia), and *Eoforwic's* defences could not prevent its capture on All Saints Day (1 November) 866. In 876, according to the *Anglo-Saxon Chronicle*, a Viking leader named Halfdene 'shared out the lands of the Northumbrians and they [the Vikings] proceeded to plough and to support themselves'. It was to be 954 before the last Scandinavian ruler was finally expelled from York. In that near century, extending from 866 to 954, the Viking *great army* settled as landlords and estate managers by right of conquest. They concentrated in southern Northumbria, between the Humber and the Tees; their kings, the politically adept archbishops, and a widening circle of merchants continued to use York as their epicentre.

There were, however, differences between Anglian *Eoforwic* and the Anglo-Scandinavian settlement which came to be called *Jorvik*. The most significant changes were the position, density and nature of occupation. Knowledge of these topics is still quite sparse, but it is certain that some areas which had been abandoned/derelict for centuries, since the Roman period, were reoccupied, while the Fishergate area was deserted (see **15**). In the Coppergate area, excavations have revealed reoccupation in the second half of the ninth century, ending over 400 years without activity. Not only reoccupation, but a carefully planned definition of properties took place. Building plots were laid out, demarcated by fence lines (**22**). These divisions, once established in the early tenth century, were to endure for a millennium, and sometimes to the present day. The dense plot layout was achieved so that a growing population could live in the city, which now covered a larger area defended partly by wholly new ramparts and timber palisades, partly by encasing the Roman walls under new earth cappings. Many of the inhabitants supported themselves by working as craftsmen, making everyday or luxury items for sale to fellow townsfolk and surrounding farmers alike. Throughout the tenth century and up to the Norman Conquest *Jorvik* was second only to London in terms both of its wealth and the size of its population.

The Scandinavian newcomers and the Northumbrian English found their way to a mutual toleration. A common bond seems to have been antagonism towards the kings of Wessex, the only English kingdom which had managed to hold out against Scandinavian takeover. Between 914 and 919 the kings of Wessex imposed domination over the lands of East Anglia, and Mercia (broadly speaking the midland counties). These territories had formerly been independent Anglo-Saxon kingdoms, rivals to Wessex; the Scandinavians had deposed their royal families, and in turn were ejected by resurgent Wessex. In 919 *Jorvik* almost came into their hands; instead, Scandinavian kings of Dublin briefly took over, instituting political links that were to recur for several generations. In 927, however, Athelstan, King of Wessex, forced his way to power in *Jorvik*; for the first time, York was part of England. His death in 939 unleashed a backlash of Scandinavian independence, and for 15 years there was a struggle for control. Eventually, after intermittent Wessex rulers, more kings from Dublin and a Norwegian prince had come and gone, kings of Wessex reaffirmed their grip on Northumbria, and after 954 *Jorvik* was never independent of English rule.

Like his distant Viking forebears, William the Conqueror had to capture the city, and like them he encountered stubborn resistance. Although *Jorvik* submitted to his troops without a fight in 1067–8, the townsfolk rebelled the very next year, but William equally quickly reasserted his grip, demonstrating his ruthless, single-minded dominance in the destruction of parts of the city. Yet York, as it came to be called in the Middle Ages, absorbed its last conquerors.

22 *16–22 Coppergate; the remains of late tenth-century buildings on each of four tenement plots. The nearest has only a stone-lined rear entrance to a still-hidden building, the others have timber walls or foundations. Scale: 2m (6ft 6in).*

23 *Bootham Bar: the eleventh-century Norman north-west gate into the medieval city with fourteenth-century turrets and heightening (the smaller arch is nineteenth-century).*

Unfortunately, few records of the early eleventh–early thirteenth centuries survive, with the result that many aspects of the Norman period and its aftermath are surprisingly mysterious. Major developments, however, have left an enduring mark. Some of the gateways in the city walls have the tell-tale round arched heads of the Norman's Romanesque style of building, and testify to an interest in strengthening the urban defences (**23**). The earthen mounds of both

William's castles still survive, one supporting the later stone keep called Clifford's Tower (see **9**), the other hidden behind a mask of trees on the opposite bank of the River Ouse. William also harnessed nature by damming the River Foss in order to strengthen the defences of the adjacent castle; the King's Pool, which formed above the dam, flooded a large low-lying area (**15**, see **24**).

If William overawed the citizens of York with military strongholds, he must have impressed them equally in his church-building. A new cathedral in the Romanesque style was built in the 1070s (**25**), replacing a Viking Age predecessor which had been burnt during the struggle for

supremacy in 1069. The substantial Norman foundations were discovered in the excavations of 1966–73 (**26, 27**). In William's wake came monks, who took over a block of land just outside the city walls and founded St Mary's Abbey, which was to become the most important monastery in northern England. Close by, the great Hospital of St Leonard was also developed.

Beyond the buildings of Church and State there are few visible traces of the Normans in York (**28**). Yet the sparse documents do indicate that, within a few decades of the conquest, York was resuming its role as not just a regional but also a national and international trading centre. The leading citizens were desperate to control their own affairs and by 1130 they had formed their own trading association; in mid-century they received a royal

24 *Reconstructed plan by Derek Phillips of twelfth-century York.*

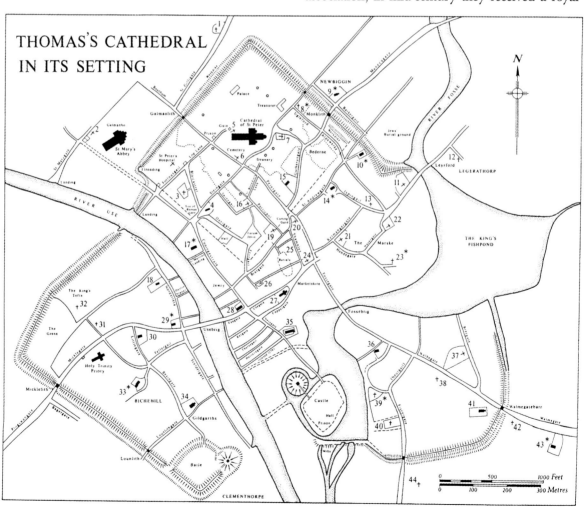

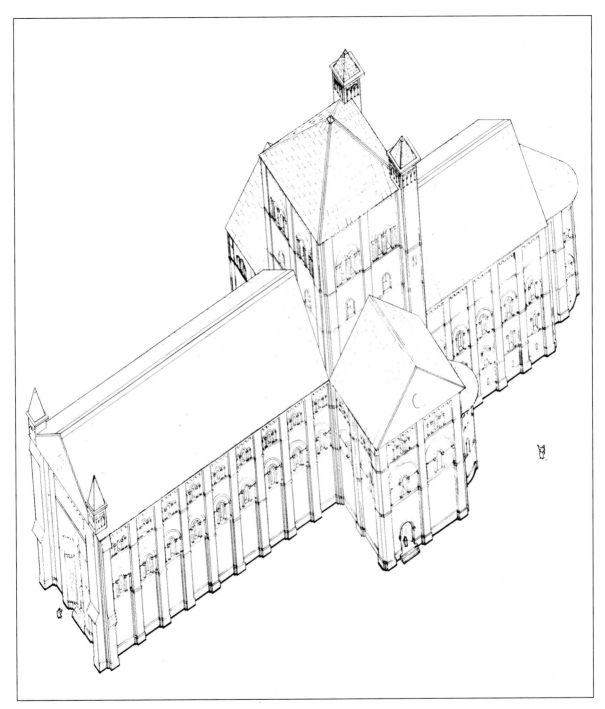

25 *Reconstruction of the later eleventh-century cathedral church, prepared under the supervision of Derek Phillips.*

charter affirming their liberties, laws and customs (**29**), by 1207 there was a civic seal (**30**), and local self-government was further assured in 1213 when King John, in return for £200, granted the citizens freedom from interference by his county sheriff. A mayor of York now represented the citizens; being a freeman of the city gave important political and commercial rights, which were still potent into the nineteenth century and which still

41

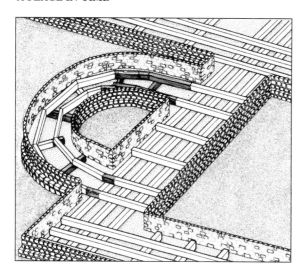

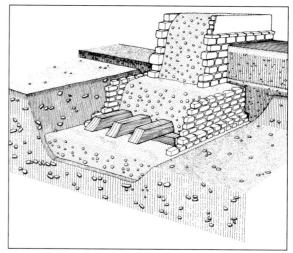

26 (Opposite left) *York Minster: reconstruction drawing of the timber grille in the foundations, using the northern apse as an example.*

27 (Opposite right) *York Minster: reconstruction drawing to show how the foundations of the late eleventh-century church were built.*

28 (Opposite below) *Norman house remains of late twelfth-century date off Stonegate.*

29 (Below) *The earliest city charter, given by Henry II, 1155–62.*

survive, in social form, today (**31**). Richard II enhanced the city's status to that of the County of the City of York in 1396; the royal castle, however, lay outside this jurisdiction (**32**).

York's prosperity continued, generally unabated, until about 1475, with wealth generated by three main areas of activity. Firstly, the city was the main administrative and judicial centre for the North of England. It housed the clerks and officials who ran the civil and ecclesiastical courts, who managed the estates, who collected the revenues and who in many other ways oiled the wheels of local and regional government. The city also catered for the flow of visitors who came to plead, to pay, or for pleasure at the metropolitan centre. There was a continuing demand for accommodation, and a spin-off for the wealthy was the opportunity to invest in property.

Secondly, York continued to be an inland port. Initially it traded directly to the Continent, but after about 1350 Hull's more convenient location near the coast made it a more popular and important North Sea dock, and most foreign goods which reached York had been trans-shipped from Hull.

30 *Impression of York City's thirteenth-century seal, reading, from top, clockwise,* +: SIGILLUM: CIVIUM: EBORACI: – *'the city seal of York'.*

43

31 *The Freemen of Micklegate Ward reserving their rights in Scarcroft Lane, giving them access from the city at Nunnery Lane to Micklegate Stray, one of the areas where they had grazing and other rights from time immemorial.*

32 *A boundary marker for the County of the City of York, at York Castle.*

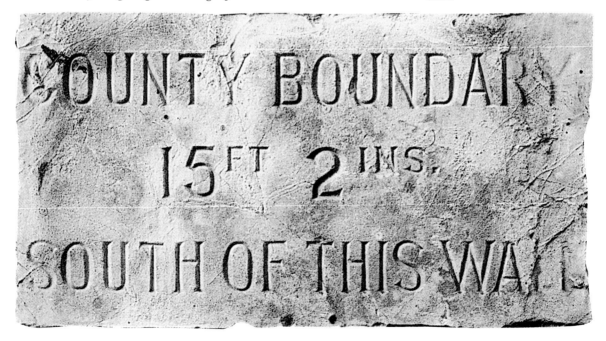

Thirdly, medieval York continued the pre-Norman role as a manufacturing centre, supplying the city and its region with a wide range of goods. There is documentary evidence for an increasingly elaborate series of craft guilds which operated in the city, and an increasing archaeological understanding of how different groups of craftsmen plied their trades.

With the growth of these activities, and a corresponding growth in population as the city acted as a magnet for the ambitious and hopeful, York changed in these centuries. Some arteries hardened – Ouse Bridge, for example, was rebuilt in stone after its timber predecessor collapsed in 1154. The city's wooden defensive palisade was replaced with stone walls c. 1250–1315 and the circuit of the city walls was expanded to include Walmgate for the first time (see 15). There was some internal replanning – Goodramgate, for example, was diverted off its direct diagonal run towards a former gateway directly behind the Minster and on to the new gate position at Monk Bar. The suburbs were also extended, sometimes gradually and sometimes with what looks like deliberate planning, as at Newbiggin.

Its historic and continuing importance, its size and prestige, and its strategic position – far enough from London to act as a counterbalance if the capital's citizens became too powerful a lobby, and near enough to Scotland to be a useful base in the continuing joust for control of the disputed border lands – kept York squarely in royal view. Henry III, for example, ordered a renovation of York Castle in the 1240s, work which included the building of a stone keep, Clifford's Tower (33, 34, 35). Furthermore, many an English king visited York. Between 1298 and 1338 Kings Edward I, II and III resided frequently in the city, bringing with them the government offices and royal courts; their main reason was to have a northern base for Scottish wars. In 1392 Richard II made York his capital for six months, getting away from the demands of Londoners, and Richard III (1483–5) also favoured York with both visits and privileges.

The city's importance faded in the 100 years between about 1450–1550, as new manufacturing and trading towns such as Wakefield, Hull and Leeds rose in significance. York's wealth declined, and the population shrank. The biggest building in York, the Minster, had been completed and dedicated in 1472 and there was no need for new civic buildings, guildhalls or parish churches. The building trades therefore declined, along with others.

The Reformation and the dissolution of the monasteries (1536–9) brought great changes to a city which had been well served with religious orders. Virtually all the monastic buildings were pulled down (36) to make way for secular redevelopments. Additionally, hospitals, chapels and several of the parish churches were shut, sold off and, usually, demolished.

After its century or so of decline, York was increasingly revitalized from 1539, when it became the seat of the King's Council in the Northern Parts. This body, housed at King's Manor, within the old St Mary's Abbey complex, governed northern England on the King's behalf until 1641. It made York a secular and judicial centre, in parallel with the church courts and administration, and brought all sorts of business to the city. Lodging houses and inns flourished, and commerce improved too, with the city's merchants reorganizing themselves into the Company of Merchant Adventurers. New buildings included magnificent town houses for the aristocracy; although none remain today, there are signs of both the taste and wealth of the times (37). When the thrones of Scotland and England were united in the person of King James I in 1603, it even seemed possible that York would become the joint nation's new, centrally placed capital; but the idea collapsed.

York was a Royalist centre in the Civil War, and Charles I had his capital here for six months in 1642. The city was besieged, bombarded and captured by the Parliamentarians in 1644. Both Royalists and Parliamentarians in turn constructed earthwork forts for their cannon outside the walled city. All traces of these have now disappeared except at Lamel Hill, on a ridge to the

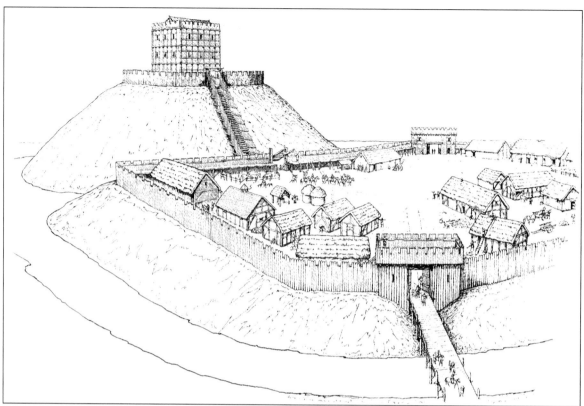

33 *Hypothetical reconstruction of York Castle in the twelfth century, with a timber tower, called Kings Tower, atop the earthen mound* (Peter Snowball).

34 *Reconstruction of York Castle* c. *1300* (Terry Ball).

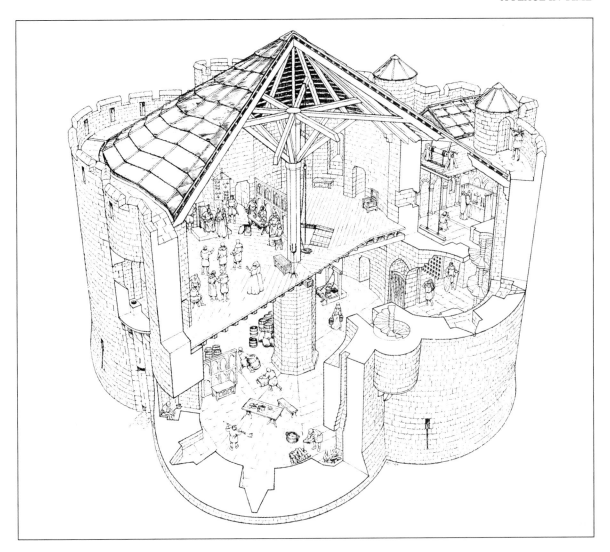

35 *Reconstructed cross-section through Clifford's Tower, the mid-thirteenth-century keep at York Castle* (Peter Snowball).

36 *From the sublime to lime – excavating the c. 1538 limekiln at Fishergate Gilbertine Priory, with the central firing chamber flanked by a flue at each side; limestone architectural fragments were turned into quicklime for use in building, agriculture or tanning.*

37 *Elaborate plasterwork of seventeenth-century date with the motto LAUS DEO ('praise to the Lord'), revealed during rebuilding at 29–31 Coney Street.*

south-east of the city, where the attackers raised a mound to bombard the Walmgate area (see **8**). Yet despite suburban damage, the city itself escaped major destruction both during and after the siege, although St Mary's Tower, Bootham, shows clearly its botched rebuilding after being undermined by the attackers (**38**).

After the Civil War York became principally a resort where the northern gentry and the well-to-do could enjoy social activities such as horse racing, or the coffee houses with their local newspapers. The city's splendid series of Georgian town houses, some obvious but others partly masked or disfigured by more recent façades, represent this aspect of York's development (**colour plate 14**). Many buildings survive from this relatively recent period; but archaeological layers so close to the modern surface have often been removed in Victorian or modern redevelopment. Archaeological excavation has therefore made rather fewer major

discoveries about this era, although there is much that could be learnt about particular aspects of life. For example, the great mansions of the age – Buckingham House in Bishophill, or Ingram's Mansion in the Dean's Park – are all but unknown.

In the eighteenth century the Castle Yard was redeveloped with the Debtors' Prison, the Assize Courts and the Female Prison. These are perhaps the most obvious of York's various civic buildings of this time. Another important building of this date is the Assembly Rooms in Blake Street, a classically inspired structure designed by Lord Burlington, which formed a suitably impressive setting for meetings of high society.

The nineteenth century saw improving communications, most notably the railway, which reached York in 1839. Parts of the first station, built within the walls, still survive. Its replacement (1869–77) (**39**) destroyed a large Roman cemetery and other buried remains; the increasing volume of railway traffic led to York being described in

38 *St Mary's Tower, Bootham, built c. 1324, part of the precinct wall of St Mary's Abbey, repaired badly after being undermined in 1644 during the Civil War.*

The East Coast Route Tourist Guide, in the early 1920s as a 'great railway centre and throbbing with the incessant whirl of modern transit'. The railway provided a reason for building a second bridge across the River Ouse, at Lendal, to give easy access to the city's heart, and a third bridge, at Skeldergate, was opened in 1881. The city centre was also opened up by the insertion of Parliament Street in 1833–6; it cut directly across the medieval tenement pattern, and was distinguished from the medieval streets by its much greater width. Other nineteenth- or early twentieth-century streets included Clifford Street, Piccadilly, Deangate, St Leonard's Place and Duncombe Place. As the railways flourished, river transport declined; looking forward, in 1919 Thomas Cook could offer air travellers access to

39 *York Station, opened 1877.*

York via an airport at Copmanthorpe, now a York suburb, but this lasted only briefly.

A small and specialized industrial base grew up during the Victorian era, in which railways and the manufacture of sweets and chocolates were most important. The gentry began to move out of the city centre, and poor working-class families, many of them Irish immigrants, moved in to what became slums in Bedern, Walmgate and in the Water Lanes area along the rivers. The slums have long gone; archaeology could probably teach us as much about living and environmental conditions in this quite recent episode as it has of the more ancient and romantic eras of York's 2000 years.

3

'One hundred per cent Anglo-Saxon with perhaps a dash of Viking'?

Tony Hancock in *The Blood Donor* (1961)

Archaeology in York is essentially a celebration of the deeds, hopes and fears of the city's inhabitants over the last 2000 years, and a crucial part of the investigation is to learn about those people themselves – who they were, where they came from, what they believed, how they lived, what they looked like. They can be approached and identified in three main ways. The first is by explicit reference to them in contemporary or near-contemporary writings. A good, although rather specialized, example is that some Viking Age kings of York are known only through the survival of the coins they issued, which bear their name. Secondly there may be characteristic objects which people, either collectively or individually, deliberately or accidentally, have left behind (**40**, see **71**; **colour plate 2**). Finally and most directly, although usually anonymously, there are human skeletal remains. Hundreds of thousands of people have lived and died in the city over the last 2000 years, and many parts of modern York are built over ancient and long-forgotten burial-grounds. The chances of encountering them today during redevelopment are quite high; if archaeologists are on hand to recover the bones carefully, their subsequent study by experts can tell much about the life-expectancy, diseases and appearance of these ancient peoples.

On the eve of the Roman advance northwards into the region, the York area was inhabited by two Iron Age tribes, the Brigantes and the Parisi. Both these peoples spoke British, one of the Celtic group of languages, and they can be described as Celtic Britons.

In AD 71 the Ninth Roman Legion, *Legio IX Hispana*, advanced from Lincoln and founded York. This force, of 5000–5500 heavy infantry together with a small number of legionary horsemen (**colour plate 1**), had been one of the legions which invaded Britain in AD 43. Immediately before the invasion they were stationed on the Danube frontier, while the name *Hispana* presumably indicates that the legion had served with distinction in the Spanish campaigns in the 20s BC.

At the time of the invasion all the legionaries were Roman citizens, about half coming from Italy, mainly northern Italy, and the other half from the western Mediterranean provinces, most from Gaul and Spain. As the normal length of service was 25 years, the only veterans of the invasion who may still have been serving with the Ninth Legion when it pushed forward to York were NCOs and officers, who served longer terms. The only officers known by name are a Spaniard and a Moesian (from the Balkans); there was also a standard bearer from Gaul. As death or discharge thinned the ranks, new recruits were drafted in, and by the later first century it was probably Roman citizens from the western provinces who made up the legion's complement. When the legionary soldiers retired, however, there was no official mechanism to transport them back to their homes, and most presumably settled down with their discharge bounty near to their last base. Thus a Romanized population quite quickly grew up around York.

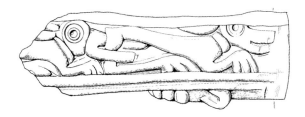

40 *Broken bone handle from 46–54 Fishergate, decorated with an interlocked animal design of c. 700. Scale: 2:1.*

One early visitor to York was Scribonius Demetrius, a Greek from Tarsus in the Roman province of Cilicia (modern south-east Turkey). In 83–4 the Roman historian Plutarch met him at Delphi, and heard about his experiences gathering military intelligence in the Western Isles, probably in 82 when the Roman general Agricola was campaigning in Scotland. Remarkably, two small bronze plaques, found in 1846 in the Toft Green area, each have a Greek inscription. One inscription translates 'To the gods of the governor's residence, Scrib[onius] Demetrius', and the other 'To Ocean and Tethys, Demetrius'. The second, appropriately for a well-educated schoolmaster with a sense of history, echoed a dedication made by Alexander the Great at the most distant part of his exploration of the Indian Ocean; Demetrius was suggesting that, at York and beyond, he was on the edge of the known world.

Eboracum remained the Ninth Legion's base until it was withdrawn from Britain in about 115–20. Into its place came *Legio VI Victrix*, the Sixth Legion Victorious, transferred from the north-west German frontier, and they retained York as their base throughout the entire Roman occupation of Britain.

As the second century went by, more and more Britons probably entered the legion, among them the sons of former legionaries. By 196, when Clodius Albinus, Governor of Britain, made a bid for control of the empire, the troops of the Sixth Legion which accompanied him to France probably included many British-born legionaries. They were defeated by the rival claimant Septimius Severus at Lyons in 197; before being sent back to *Eboracum* the remnant of the Sixth was reinforced with troops loyal to Severus. The new emperor himself was North African, and it has recently become clear that the new blood transferred into the legion were also North Africans, from the area of modern Libya, Tunisia, Algeria and Morocco. They can be identified in York by their distinctive pottery types, which closely resemble the native pottery of those regions (**41**). The funerary practice of plaster burials, which occurs in York (p. 101),

41 *Pottery types from York which are modelled on North African wares. Scale: 1:4.*

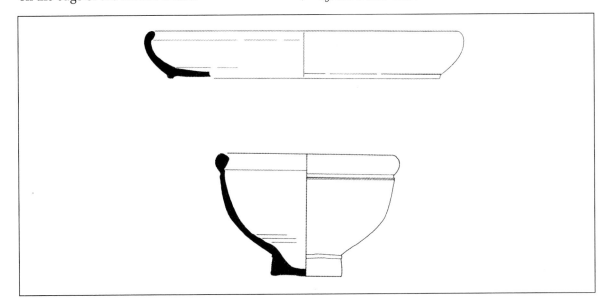

also originated in North Africa; its introduction to York might be due to this new component in the ranks of the Sixth. It has even been suggested that some attributes of skeletons from a Roman cemetery excavated at Trentholme Drive, including skull features, limb proportions and distinctive dental indices, indicate the occasional presence of people with negroid features.

Another occasion for the arrival of Africans in York was the period 208–11 when Severus made *Eboracum* the imperial capital while he campaigned against the Scottish tribes. He certainly brought his Syrian wife Julia Domna with him, as well as his sons Caracalla and Geta, and his imperial household which included other North Africans in senior positions. One archaeological result of this presence was the so-called head pots which were made in York at this time, probably for religious votive offerings. Most feature a woman's face, and the distinctive hairstyle suggests it was the Empress Julia Domna who acted as inspiration (**42**). Another unusual glimpse of fashionable *coiffure* comes occasionally when an individual's hair is preserved in the grave along with their skeleton. Instances at York which are clearly Roman in date include one woman with auburn hair in ringlets, and an adolescent girl whose auburn hair was held in a bun by two jet hairpins.

A religious dedication stone erected in York by a helmsman or pilot of the Sixth Legion appeals to the mother goddesses of Africa, Italy and Gaul, and this suggests that the Legion included men from all those areas. Distinctive pottery types parallelled in south-western Provence and Languedoc confirm that potters from southern France, probably in the Legion, were based in York. Altogether, in the years around 200 York must have been a cosmopolitan centre.

In the third and fourth centuries the Sixth Legion may well have consisted largely of British-born troops, although it is more likely that officers were posted in from other parts of the empire. There certainly were occasions when an influx of foreigners descended upon York. When the emperor Constantius I died in York in 306, his son Constantine was proclaimed as successor

42 *Third-century face pot, found in York Cemetery in 1888. Height: 0.3m (11¾in)* (Reproduced by courtesy of the Yorkshire Museum).

by a German leader called Crocus. He belonged to the Alemanni, a tribe which occupied what is now southern Germany, directly across the Romans' Rhine and Danube frontier. Constantius had suppressed the Alemanni in a series of campaigns just before he came to Britain; presumably an Alemannic detachment had been forced to join the Emperor, and had accompanied him across the North Sea. Crocus and his Alemanni are just the most historically visible, and also among the latest, of any number of non-legionary troops who may have passed through *Eboracum* on their way to postings to forts and bases on or near the northern frontier. Soldiers from what are now France, Germany, Spain, the Balkans and even Syria were among those who served in north Britain.

Many legionaries must have literally shacked up with local girls, and raised families; their sons are likely to have followed them into Roman military service. In the first and second centuries, at least, there were probably rather mixed blood-lines and an exotic gene pool in the surrounds of *Eboracum*, but how far this may have extended into the wider tribal territories is uncertain, for there was a continuing numerical predominance of British Celts in the area.

The other element in the population of *Eboracum* was the residents of the civilian settlements around the fortress. In one way or another they were dependent on the soldiery for a living. Initially, camp-followers and private suppliers would have come from south of the Humber, either from among the Britons or, if the market warranted, from abroad. With time, more local Britons probably jumped on this relatively lucrative bandwagon. It is likely too that there was a wide range of social types among these people

with everything from pimps and shady dealers at one end of the range to the *nouveaux riches* and British gentry at the other. It is the well-to-do who are easier to recognize, for example by their luxuriously decorated houses and their ostentatious religious devotion. We know of the *negotiator* (rich merchant) Lucius Viducius Placidus, who traded at both Rouen and York, because he was rich enough to commission and erect a dedicatory inscription which has immortalized him (**43**).

We can get close to some families and individuals through the biographical information on their tombstones or their coffins. Burials with memorials of this type are the exception rather than the rule, the prerogative of the relatively

43 *Latin dedicatory inscription of AD 221 found at Clementhorpe, damaged at the left edge. It was erected by L[UCIUS] VIDUCIUS [PLA]CIDUS whose name is on the second and third lines; three lines from the bottom the word [N]EGOTIATOR indicates he was a merchant.*

well-to-do. Such people may not be typical citizens of *Eboracum*. Yet they do represent an interesting element of that population, and they are the *only* Roman residents documented in this way – indeed such a collection of potted biographies becomes available again only from the seventeenth century.

Often the inscriptions tell something of the religious leanings of the deceased. Occasionally, their home town or region is given: Julia Fortunata, for example, died in York but originated in Sardinia. Her husband, Marcus Verecundius Diogenes, a *sevir* (see p. 15), came from Bourges. Lucius Duccius Rufinus, a standard bearer in the Ninth Legion, originated in Vienne; Lucius Baebius Crescens, a soldier in the Sixth Legion, was from Augsburg.

Some dozen or so inscriptions provide information on the individual's lifespan. Here there is an immediate contrast with modern expectations. None of these people lived beyond 50 years of age; the oldest man, a soldier with 23 years' service in the Sixth Legion, died aged 43. There are several instances where a mother and child were commemorated together: Eglecta (30) and her three-year-old son; Flavia Augustina (39), the wife of a legionary veteran, with two children aged 12 months and 21 months; Julia Brica (31) and her six-year-old daughter; Julia Victorina (29), a centurion's wife, and her son aged four. Some inscriptions refer only to infants or children: for example, Simplicia Florentina, who died aged ten months, commemorated by her soldier father. The grief which accompanied the death of Corellia Optata (13) was echoed in her funerary inscription: 'I, the pitiable father of an innocent daughter, caught by cheating hope, lament her final end . . .'

These inscriptions indicate that life for residents of *Eboracum* was relatively short and uncertain; that when a Roman drinking cup carrying the motto *Vivatis* – 'Long life to you' – was raised in a toast, the realistic drinker was looking forward to just a few decades more. The question is, are these inscriptions a reliable guide to average expectations, or a small and biased sample? To answer this, the only form of evidence potentially available in large quantities is skeletal remains.

In spite of the very large numbers of Roman burials which have been found in York – hundreds to which there is some reference, however slight, and probably thousands wholly unrecorded – very few have been excavated scientifically and then studied by experts. The largest sample is about 350 skeletons and the remains of over 50 cremations which were recovered in excavations undertaken by Peter Wenham in the 1950s at Trentholme Drive, off The Mount, the main approach to York from the south. This area was used as a cemetery from the mid-second to mid-fourth century. It was probably the poorer sections of the community who were buried here, for there was a general absence of expensive or luxurious grave goods. The only other groups of Roman burials discovered since are the 31 excavated by YAT at 35–41 Blossom Street, only 160m (175 yds) from the hypothetical perimeter line of the *colonia*, and six burials of late third- to mid-fourth-century date from 16–22 Coppergate, just 160m (175 yds) south-east of the Roman fortress wall. This number, spread in time and social class, is hardly representative of the population of *Eboracum*. As with the funerary inscriptions, however, these are all the data there are, and their analysis may provide at least pointers to facets of ancient life.

Taking the Trentholme Drive skeletons as a single group, and thus assuming that no great changes occurred during the centuries which the cemetery spanned, the indications about life-expectancy given in the inscriptions are broadly confirmed. About 7½ per cent of the individuals interred had died before reaching 15 years of age, and another 7½ per cent succumbed before they were 20. As much as 50 per cent of the population died between the ages of 20 and 40, leaving only 35 per cent to enter their fifth decade.

The doubt that nags the archaeologist here is the knowledge that children's bones, particularly those of babies and infants, are very small and correspondingly fragile. They are therefore most likely to disappear from the archaeological record, either through natural processes of decay or because their traces may be overlooked during excavation. Perhaps, too, the bodies of neonates/infants were treated differently to those of older children and adults, and are not so easy to discover. It was a surprise, for example, to find one such burial in the construction layers of a military building in the fortress at 9 Blake Street (now the Stonegate Arcade), and another example was found in the York Minster excavations. Even later, in the nominally Christian seventh–ninth centuries, babies' bones have been found in rubbish pits at Fishergate. Probably, therefore, infant mortality was higher, perhaps much higher, than the cemetery statistics suggest.

In the Trentholme Drive cemetery average male height was 1.70m (5ft 7in) while women averaged 1.55m (5ft 1in). Individuals of both sexes were often strong and stocky, as if used to hard physical work, and they suffered a range of medical conditions which had left marks on their skeletons. Various osteoarthritic ailments were quite usual, and fractures of arms or legs, hands or feet were not uncommon. There was even a single case of trephining, where a piece of the skull had been carefully removed, presumably in the hope of alleviating a pain in the head. Dental diseases had apparently not proved particular problems for most people, and dental caries became a noticeable factor only for individuals who had reached the 35–40 age group.

Other insights into the health of *Eboracum*'s citizens come from less obvious sources. A tiny stamp or mould for marking cakes of ointment, found in The Mount area south of the *colonia*, has an inscription which translates as 'Julius Alexander's salve for irritations'; experts identify this as evidence for an oculist treating eye complaints. At the other end of the body, a study of about 150 Roman leather shoes excavated at Tanner Row has revealed chiropodical and anatomical problems which their owners suffered. Unusual wear and repair patterns show, for example, that there were cases of high arched foot, which could lead to painful callousing and

corns. Bunions and flat feet were also represented, and overall this admittedly small sample suggests that foot problems were much more common than today.

Information of another sort has come from an accumulation of sediments in a Roman drain at Tanner Row, which is in the *colonia*. Human faeces in the drain had contained the eggs of gut worms which live as parasites in the human intestines. These worms were a burden for at least some of York's population until the nineteenth or even the early twentieth century, for only improved water supply, sanitation and hygiene has eradicated them. As successful parasites, however, they won't have unduly affected their human hosts.

The next population influx that we know of is that of the Anglo-Saxons who started to settle in England during the fifth century. These peoples, predominantly from Holland, north Germany and Denmark, are recognized in the archaeological record through their characteristic cremation urns and through the forms of jewellery, weapons and other objects found in their inhumation graves. Both the pots and other artefacts found in their Northumbrian graves are most closely matched in modern Schleswig-Holstein and the Danish islands, the area anciently known as Angeln, and this indicates that the settlers here were mainly Angles rather than Saxons or Jutes. The grave goods make it clear that women as well as men crossed the North Sea, but it is difficult to estimate how many Germanic immigrants lived in the vicinity of York.

The allied problem is to gauge the relationships between the immigrants and the resident Britons. Was the conquest achieved by relatively small bands of intruders who struck decisive military blows but then dominated by skilful diplomacy? Was it an overwhelming force of arms which subdued the Britons of Northumbria? Or was it largely a peaceful settlement and assimilation? The traditional means of estimating numbers has been to count characteristic burials, but this has now been recognized as potentially misleading. It may, after all, have become fashionable (or 'politically correct', with all the social overtones of that phrase) for Britons to imitate the funerary customs of the new Anglian aristocracy – a case of follow my (new) leader. One day it may be possible to determine whether overtly Anglian burials are those of Britons or Angles by DNA testing of the bones.

Even if all the distinctively 'Anglian' graves did contain an ethnic German rather than a Briton, there are still very few of them from York, and this is equally true in relative terms for the whole of Northumbria (and true also for the graves of Britons). It seems therefore that there was always a majority of people descended from Britons in the 'Anglian period' population both of Yorkshire and of *Eoforwic*.

There were, of course, people of other nationalities in *Eoforwic*. In the early seventh century, the first missionary to bring Roman Christianity from its English foothold in Kent was Paulinus, an Italian monk, remembered as tall, stooping slightly, with black hair, a thin hooked nose and thin face. And in 685 the eighty-or-more-year-old Greek-speaking intellectual, Theodore of Tarsus, from Cilicia in modern Turkey, came to York in his role as Archbishop of Canterbury, to consecrate (St) Cuthbert as a bishop. *Eoforwic* also attracted foreign merchants. Goods from northern France, the Low Countries and the Rhineland indicate the activities of traders from those areas. Although it might be argued that these exotic items were channelled through a more restricted group of local middlemen, the fact that some of the imported pottery is in forms which are more appropriate for domestic rather than commercial use supports the presence of foreigners.

One marvellous archaeological discovery shows clearly that people of the highest status were present in *Eoforwic* (**44,colour plate 5**). It is an iron helmet with brass embellishments, found thanks to an amazing chance during the building of the Coppergate Centre, about 10m (33ft) from the limits of the long-running excavation there, and only a few centimetres (an inch) below the base of a Victorian chimney stack. Richly decorated with animal ornamentation on the

44 *The Coppergate Anglian helmet, c. 750–75.*

noseguard and eyebrows, and with a religious inscription on the strips quartering the skull, perhaps its most impressive feature is the mail neck protector. This is made of about 2000 tiny links with alternate rows welded and rivetted in a technical *tour-de-force*. The effort in its production shouts wealth, influence, patronage: if the Oshere named in the inscription was its owner, Oshere was a rich and powerful aristocrat in late eighth-century *Eoforwic*.

Further complicating the picture is the invasion and settlement of Viking warriors in the late ninth century. Defining this Scandinavian presence is fraught with difficulties. Some of the uncertainties echo those surrounding the Anglo-Saxons – particularly in terms of how many Scandinavians actually settled in and around York. How many men were part of a *great army* in ninth-century terms? In Anglo-Saxon law, an army was anything upwards of 35 men – so a *great army* needn't have been very big. Yet it did have to hold off a Northumbrian counter-attack which would, in theory, have been numerically quite strong. But since, as Napoleon remarked, the moral is to the physical as three is to one, and as the Northumbrians had already been defeated by the Vikings, numbers may not have been everything in this fight, and the result can't be readily turned into some sort of mathematical equation. Common sense suggests that the Viking army in York must have been several, perhaps many, hundreds strong, but we'll probably never know. Equally, we can't be sure whether or not there was a secondary immigration from Scandinavia to York and Yorkshire after the initial conquest, and whether such a move involved predominantly men, or families, or included unaccompanied/unchaperoned women.

Certainly we can't estimate on the basis of the discovery of recognizable Viking burials. Although the invading Vikings were not Christians, and buried their dead with characteristic weapons, jewellery, etc., only two human skeletons laid in the ground together with grave

goods of identifiably Viking type have ever been found in York. Perversely, this scarcity may be because the conquering Vikings adopted the burial habits of the Anglians and became virtually indistinguishable from them in the grave. Once again, future DNA testing may unravel this story.

To the English, the Viking *great army* was Danish in origin, but place-names in York's hinterland which have Old Norse elements, and which were presumably given in the wake of the Scandinavian settlement, include not only Danby – 'the settlement of the Danes' – but also Normanby – 'the settlement of the Norwegians'. The place name Uppsall, a variant of Swedish Upsalla, is one of several pieces of evidence which suggests that some Swedes were also present. There is some evidence, principally in the form of place names and art styles, that Hiberno-Norsemen (Scandinavians with Irish connections) settled in Yorkshire and thus, perhaps, in York itself, and the names of the moneyers responsible for striking York's coinage *c.* 900–50 suggest that several of them were of continental origin.

The most famous invasion in British history, the Norman Conquest, initially placed a foreign garrison of 500 knights at York in the midst of a hostile populace. 'Domesday Book' indicates some of the administrative roles played by the Normans in the decades immediately after they seized power, and also gives the names of great Norman landowners, but of course it does not tell us how many lesser Normans settled in York.

One mysterious change in the people of York which has sometimes been linked to the Normans' arrival is an alteration in skull type and thus in physical appearance. The evidence comes from an assessment of over 1000 burials from the church and churchyard of St Helen-on-the-Walls, in Aldwark, excavated by YAT in 1973–6; later excavations of what is believed to be the eleventh- and twelfth-century church of St Andrew in Fishergate, and the later medieval Gilbertine Priory on the same site, confirmed this anatomical trend. The basic change was a slight but significant lessening in the length of the face, whilst the width remained broadly constant. This phenomenon is not unique to York – it has been recognized at the deserted medieval village of Wharram Percy, on the Yorkshire Wolds 29km (18 miles) north-east of York, and more recently in Ipswich. How closely such a change can be linked to the Normans is in fact questionable, for the dating of these burials is not very precise, and the rate of change not at all clear. The reasons for change are not understood either, although in what would be a classic example of the aphorism 'You are what you eat', alteration in basic diet has been one tentative suggestion.

It is known that it wasn't simply men from Normandy who had followed William the Conqueror to England and to York, and among the 20 or so Frenchmen who held 145 properties in 1086 there may have been other continentals. It is certainly tempting to think that there may have been some Bretons living in York in the wake of the Norman Conquest – this would account for the *'bret'* element in the surviving street name Jubbergate (earlier *Brettegate*) and in another, now discarded street name, Little Bretgate. It has been traditional to think that these name elements indicate that Britons, either descendants of the native, pre-Anglo-Scandinavian population, or the later, Viking Age population of Cumbria, were a recognizable element in the pre-Norman city, living in the vicinity of these streets, and giving their names to them. But as *-gate* names continued to be coined in York well after the Norman Conquest (most obviously demonstrated by the name Castle-gate – there was no castle in York before the Normans), it is possible that the *bret* names are also Norman.

Parallel to *Brettegate*, in what was Girdlergate and is now Church Street, lies the church of St Sampson, a sixth-century Welsh saint associated with Dol in Brittany. Advocates of a British enclave in Anglian or Anglo-Scandinavian York point to the dedication to the British saint Sampson as bolstering their argument. The fact that the church is first recorded in 1154 may not seem to support its being an early foundation, but this could arguably reflect the scarcity of early documentation; yet perhaps the coincidence of *Brettegate* and St Sampson's Church points to a Breton presence in twelfth-century York.

The 'Ju' element in *Jubbergate* introduces another, slightly better-known, element in the population of Anglo-Norman York – the Jews. A Jewish community seems to have grown up during the reign of Henry II (1154–89), perhaps in the early 1170s. Although several were prominent figures nationally, never mind locally, the community was still quite a small one – estimates hover around the 150 mark, perhaps equating to 20–40 households. Property deeds show that many Jews lived in Jubbergate and in Coney Streeet, where their synagogue was. Their community was more or less wiped out in their mass suicide at York castle in 1190 when taking refuge from a Christian mob incited by religious and financial concerns, but within a few years other Jews had arrived in York. The community reached its zenith, at perhaps 200 or more individuals, in the period *c.* 1220–60 before declining to just six households until expelled from the country, along with all other English Jews, in 1290.

Excavation at Jewbury, just outside the city walls, in 1982–3, confirmed that this was indeed the burial-ground of the medieval Jewish population. Study of their bones revealed that although they were what is termed a 'religious isolate' – that is, a closed community who did not intermarry with non-Jewish citizens – they were physically virtually inseparable from their Christian neighbours. In terms of cranial and facial character Jews were not particularly distinctive overall in York's population, but some would have stood out with relatively long faces and high eye sockets. They were also slightly shorter than their Christian contemporaries with males averaging 1.67m (5ft 5¾ in) and females 1.56m (5ft 1½ in), but they seem to have been less prone to injury, with, for example, a relatively low number of fractures to their long bones. One skull showed a remarkable early example of surgery. The individual had suffered a deep cut which would have damaged the brain, but which did not cause immediate death. The wound had been opened up for cleaning purposes, cutting the bone back to remove bone splinters or whatever had caused the injury. Yet despite, or perhaps because of this, the patient did not survive for long – there was no remedial growth of the bone.

From the perspective of some southern English writers of this period, York was only just within the boundaries of civilization. William of Malmesbury, writing *c.* 1125, noted that 'almost everything about the language of the North, and particularly of the population of York, is so crude and discordant that we southerners cannot understand it. This is because they are near to barbarian peoples . . .' In similar vein, perhaps, Richard of Devizes noted that the city was 'full of Scotsmen, filthy and treacherous creatures, scarcely human'.

In the thirteenth and fourteenth centuries it is clear that York was a Mecca for Yorkshiremen who thought it provided opportunities to do better in life. Personal names such as Peter of Foxholes or James of Pickering, which occur in the earliest surviving register of citizens, proclaim the story of regional incomers; but York's net was spread wider, at least as far as the Low Countries – James the Fleming was Mayor in 1298, and Nicholas the Fleming Mayor on several occasions between 1311 and 1319.

In contrast with the Anglian and Viking Age periods, it has been possible to study the population of medieval York, for the excavations at St Helen-on-the-Walls in Aldwark, and at St Andrews in Fishergate, have presented opportunities for skeletal analysis. In both cases the cemetery seems to have originated round about the year 1000, and the graveyards were closed in the mid-sixteenth century. The skeletons from St Andrew's form two distinct groups, the earlier (eleventh–twelfth century) parishioners, and the later (thirteenth–mid-sixteenth century) canons and patrons of the Priory; the different social and economic circumstances of the two groups may well have influenced not only their lives but also their skeletons.

Among both sets of parishioners, about 35 per cent died before reaching adulthood at about 20 years of age. More than half of this number did not survive their fifth birthday. At

45 *Copper-alloy plates found at the knee of a late medieval burial at the Gilbertine priory, Fishergate. Scale: 0.2m (8in).*

St Helen-on-the-Walls, 56 per cent of adult women died before they reached 35, compared to only 36 per cent of adult men, presumably as a result of the rigours and dangers of childbirth. The figures for the eleventh- to twelfth-century Fishergate parish cemetery were calculated in a slightly different way, and show that about 35 per cent of adult women died aged 20–30, nearly 20 per cent at 30–40, and just over 40 per cent at 40–50. Among males the comparable statistics were 50 per cent, 30 percent and 13½ per cent; but the number of younger males is exaggerated by the presence here of individuals with battle injuries.

Reverting to appearance, the Fishergate evidence is that women's average height was about 1.58m (5ft 2¼in) in the eleventh–twelfth centuries and 1.59m (5ft 2½in) in the thirteenth–sixteenth centuries (1.57m (5ft 1¾ins) at St Helen's), while males were 1.72m (5ft 7¾in) in the eleventh – twelfth centuries and 1.71m (5ft 7¾in) in the thirteenth–sixteenth centuries (1.69m (5ft 6½in) at St Helen's). Degenerative joint disease was quite common, most often in the spine. In one unusual case at St Andrew's, a defective right knee joint was treated by somehow holding two copper-alloy plates in position (45). It has been suggested that they supplied support and/or acted as a therapeutic treatment, combining the cleansing or suppurative

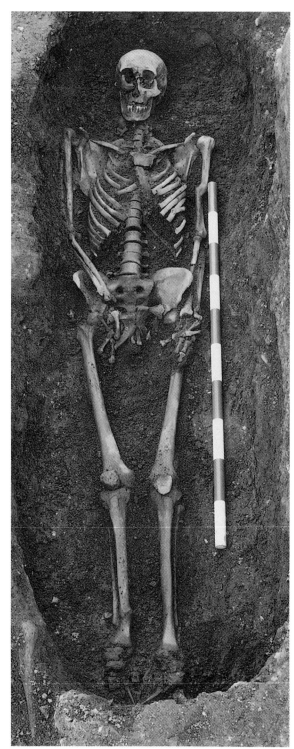

46 *A late medieval male, aged 35–45 years, buried at St Helen-on-the-Walls, Aldwark, with healed fractures of both his upper arms and all four lower leg bones.*

47 *Lady Row, Goodramgate, built in 1316; York's earliest surviving secular buildings still in use.*

effect of the copper with a herbal poultice. Broken bones were also a commonplace of medieval life. Rib fractures were most usual, and broken vertebrae in the spine also fairly frequent; as might be expected, broken arms, legs, ankles, feet, fingers, shoulder blades, and collar bones were also recorded, as well as a fractured skull. A single skeleton at St Helen's had six broken bones – both upper arms and all four bones in the lower legs. All were badly set, but had healed without infection (**46**). It looks as if the individual had been run over by a cart – a medieval traffic accident!

As with all previous generations of Yorkers, we can appreciate something of the mentality of these people through a knowledge of their everyday surrounds. The houses they lived in sometimes survive – the earliest intact examples are Lady Row, Goodramgate, erected in 1316 (**47**), but more and larger examples remain from the fifteenth and sixteenth centuries. Occasionally, the floors and foundations of contemporary buildings are investigated when redevelopment removes modern, masking structures; a good example of the laying bare of a whole streetscape is the excavations in Swinegate

48 *Late medieval building foundations at Back Swinegate, emphasizing that fine timber-framed buildings leave relatively slight and vulnerable archaeological remains. Scale: 2m (6ft 6in).*

49 *Excavating the impression of a fifteenth-century tiled floor round a central hearth at Barley Hall, Coffee Yard.*

and Back Swinegate in 1989 (**48**). In one unique instance, in nearby Coffee Yard, it's been possible both to study a fourteenth- to fifteenth-century house as it was dismantled for repair and restoration, to take the opportunity to excavate within and around it (**49**), and then to marry the archaeological data with contemporary documentation. Its later history also shows what could happen to such houses: subdivided and sublet, it eventually became a warren of small rooms, with floors inserted in the Great Hall and Great Chamber, part of the roof lowered, and extra rooms tacked on; during this dismembering the screens passage, which had once divided the Hall from the service rooms, became a public right of way, and so it remains (**50**). But within all this the original form of the building, now known as Barley Hall, has been revealed as it was in 1483 (**51**) when it was occupied by William Snawshell, a leading York citizen, goldsmith and

50 *Reconstructed fifteenth-century Great Hall wing of Barley Hall in Coffee Yard: the screens passage is now a public right of way.*

51 *Reconstruction of the timber framing of fourteenth- and fifteenth-century date at Barley Hall, Coffee Yard.*

Mayor. With its well-appointed main rooms, it reveals the relative opulence available to prosperous citizens (**colour plate 11**).

One unusual item, found in those Swinegate excavations. which gives a particularly sharp insight into its owner is a set of eight small (30mm x 50mm) wax tablets (**52**), the equivalent *c.* 1350 of a pocket notebook or personal organizer. Three different texts had been inscribed on

52 *Inscribed wax tablets, dated c. 1375–1400, from Back Swinegate. Each measures 30mm x 50mm (1¼in x 2in).*

1 *Early second-century cavalryman at* Eboracum *(Simon Chew)*.

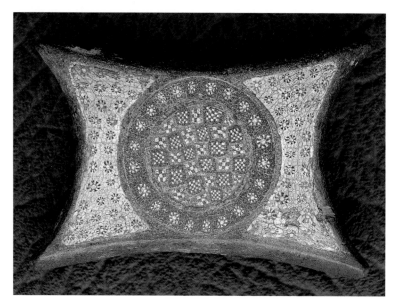

2 *Enamelled military belt-plaque, c. AD 100–50, found at 9 Blake Street. Length: 56mm (2⅛ ins).*

3 *Cornelian gemstone from a Roman ring found at 16–22 Coppergate, engraved with a charioteer, perhaps representing the god Mars. Length: 19mm (¾ in).*

4 *Eighth-century copper-alloy cross brooch, originally inlaid with red and yellow enamel, found at Paragon Street. Width: 25mm (1in).*

5 *The Coppergate Anglian helmet, c. 750–75.*

6 *Painted coffin lid of Archbishop Walter de Gray (died 1255), from his tomb in York Minster.*

7 and 8 *Opulence among the Vicars Choral at Bedern? A gold and sapphire finger-ring, diam.: 19mm (¾ in), and a gold brooch, diam.: 16mm (⅝ in).*

9 *St Denys, Walmgate: the mid-fourteenth-century donor of a window, perhaps Robert de Skelton, commemorated upon it.*

10 *Details from the early fifteenth-century 'Pricke of Conscience' window in All Saints, North Street – apocalyptic scenes from the Fifteen Last Days of the World.* Bottom left *(day eleven): People come out of hiding.* Bottom right *(day twelve): The dead arise.* Top left *(day fourteen): Death of all people.* Top right *(day fifteen): Universal fire.*

11 *Barley Hall, Coffee Yard: the reconstructed fifteenth-century Great Hall, looking across the hearth towards the high table.*

12 *W. Marlow, Old Ouse Bridge (c. 1763).*

13 *Excavation of a post-medieval bakery at the Bedern, with a medieval cityscape behind.*

14 *Georgian splendour: Castlegate House, designed by John Carr, built 1762–3.*

15 *A barge with newsprint for the York & County Press negotiates the 1811 Foss Bridge, designed by Peter Atkinson Junior.*

16 *Leethams flour mill on the river Foss, designed by W. G. Penty, 1895–6.*

the wax leaves. One is a legal document, written in Latin; the second seems to be a set of accounts. But the lighter side of life shines through in the third, a prose poem written in Middle English. The full text of this work has yet to be puzzled out, but its music-hall flavour is made crystal-clear in the recurrent phrase 'She said to me nothing not no', which could be updated as 'She didn't say yes, but she didn't say no'!

In more recent times the rather mixed community of late medieval York was further added to by the arrival of some Huguenot (French Protestant) refugees in the later eighteenth century, and by a wave of Irish emigrants in the 1840s, fleeing the Great Famine. Movement to and fro, in and out, has obviously been a hallmark in York's development; yet for some there is a feeling of permanence. When YAT found the late eleventh-/twelfth-century seal of Snarrus the tollkeeper, a phone call the next day began 'I see you've found my ancestor's seal; I'll come round tomorrow to collect it' (53). In fact, the title to possession could not be proven – but there is still a brace of Snarrs in the York telephone directory.

53 *Ivory seal, late eleventh-/twelfth century, found at Aldwark, showing a man holding a purse with three coins falling into it. Starting at the top and reading anti-clockwise, the reversed inscription is + SIG +. SNARRI. THEOLENARII. – 'the seal of Snarrus the toll collector'. Diam.: 38mm (1½ in).*

4
The urban environment

York's commanding position in the regional land-scape has already been introduced (p. 25); excavations in St George's Fields, the tip of the tongue of land between the rivers Ouse and Foss, show in detail how the area has developed since the last Ice Age. About 10m (33 ft) below present ground surface is a layer of clay, probably deposited as the glaciers melted away. Above are layers of sand and gravel, laid down by rivers which did not have well-defined channels. With time, layers of finer water-borne alluvium covered the gravels, and woodland developed as far as the water's edge. Mosses, leaves and tree-trunks were preserved in the waterlogged layers, as well as associated insect remains, and have been dated by the radio-carbon technique to the mid- to late Bronze Age, c. 1100 BC. The insect species, some of which are now rare or extinct in northern England, were mainly woodland, marshland and aquatic dwellers; the aquatic species were mostly those which prefer still rather than flowing water. Identification of the plant and tree species confirmed that the immediate area was a mosaic of alder carr interspersed with shallow pools of water. There were also insects normally associated with pasture or the dung of domestic animals, showing that animal husbandry must have been practised nearby. This landscape was itself covered up by centuries of further alluvial deposits which continued to raise the ground level until it reached the present level by the medieval period.

The Romans' impact on York's topography and environment was instantly dramatic,

although only now is it gradually being pieced together. The general area suitable for their fortress seems to have been quite flat, and probably needed only the removal of grass, trees and shrubs before building began. The precise position of the central gateway at the river frontage, and thus of the whole symmetrical layout, seems to have been determined by the best place for the bridge across the Ouse. Although it is not obvious today, the Ouse narrowed appreciably, just beyond where Tanner Row approaches the river. The Romans chose this as the easiest place to build their bridgehead. Although no definite trace of it has ever been found, the approach road, which was just to the west of Tanner Row, has been discovered in excavations.

In the few parts of the fortress which have been excavated it is striking how remarkably clean and tidy the place was until the fourth century, at least by comparison with the medieval period. This clean living shows itself in a general absence of rubbish dumps and even of rubbish pits and cesspits. Everyday waste and debris were presumably carted outside the fortress for disposal. The nature of the Roman military buildings also made it relatively easy to keep them clean. Although in the late first and even early second centuries many buildings were of timber construction, with walls consisting of vertical posts, and the gaps between them infilled with clay, possibly supported by wattlework panels, their roofs were apparently of tile. This made them weatherproof and longer-lasting than thatched buildings. By the mid to late second century all had been replaced with stone structures, often with cement floors and plastered walls, and the streets were stone- or cobble-paved. Good military discipline presumably contributed to the maintenance of standards of cleanliness. However, there does seem to have been some change in the later third and fourth century, when debris was allowed to build up both on the roads as well as within and around buildings.

The Romans also introduced a water supply, drains and sewers to the fortress area. In at least one place, below York Minster, a Roman drain has been unblocked and still functions, taking water away from the foundations. Elsewhere, analysis of the insects and pollen found in the outflow channel from the military bath-house, below Swinegate (**54**), has revealed that the water must have flowed into the fortress along a closed aqueduct from a spring in an area of mixed oak woodland. The sewer system became blocked in the late fourth/early fifth century; by the twelfth century Swinegate and its eastern continuation were both known as Patrick Pool, and it has been suggested that the pool was created by water channelled down the Roman sewer, but this seems unlikely. More probably, the rampart and stone wall of the fortress helped to create an impervious barrier which held back ground water.

Across the Ouse, in the civilian town, the Roman impact is more obvious, at least to the archaeologist, for the pronounced natural slope down to the river demanded greater intervention. Ditches, which probably acted both as plot divisions and drainage channels, were dug early. In the later second century, level building platforms were created in some places by dumping layers of turf and clay to counteract the natural slope, and in the early third century this problem was solved in part of the eastern end of the *colonia* by creating a terrace approximately midway down the slope.

Overall, however, the Roman street layout has not survived so well in the *colonia* as in the fortress. The 1980s brought confirmation that a

54 *Swinegate Roman sewer inspected in 1972 by Peter Addyman, Director of York Archaeological Trust.*

main spinal street ran straight down the valley slope to the Roman bridgehead facing the centre of the fortress. Today the uppermost length of this street is reflected (approximately) in the course of Micklegate as it runs from Micklegate Bar to Barker Lane; the bottom stretch is approximated to by Tanner Row. The middle section of the Roman road is completely obliterated and little of the remainder of the Roman street plan or block layout can be recognized today (**55**).

Along the River Ouse, remains of a riverside road or hard-standing were recorded in excavation at Skeldergate in 1974. Further information came when excavation at North Street in 1993 uncovered for the first time evidence for a wall, of second-century date, at or near the waterfront. Its base was at 1.95m (6ft 4in) above Ordnance

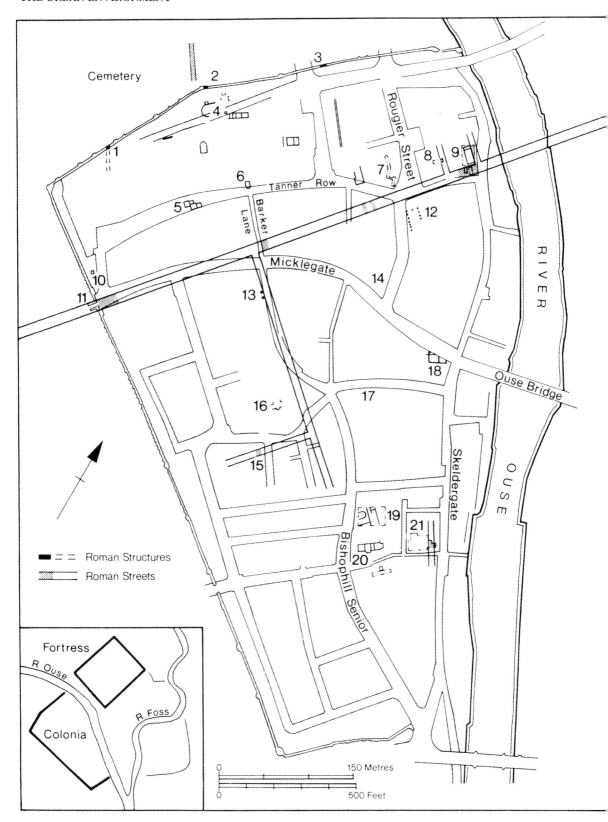

Cemetery

Rougier Street

Tanner Row

Barker Lane

Micklegate

RIVER

Ouse Bridge

Skeldergate

OUSE

Bishophill Senior

■ = = Roman Structures

Roman Streets

Fortress

R. Ouse

R. Foss

Colonia

0   150 Metres

0   500 Feet

55 *The Roman civilian settlement at the south-west bank of the Ouse showing the location of archaeological discoveries, principal excavations and streets (known and conjectured).*

1 Old Station: defences
2 Old Station: defences
3 Old Station: defences and Mithraic (Arimanius) relief
4 Old Station: baths
5 Toft Green: mosaics
6 Temple of Serapis
7 General Accident, Tanner Row: buildings
8 5 Rougier Street: warehouse and street
9 Wellington Row: main road and building
10 Barker Lane: mosaic
11 Micklegate Bar
12 George Hudson Street: column bases of ?temple or forum basilica
13 Trinity Lane: column bases
14 Micklegate / George Hudson Street: Mithraic relief and column bases
15 Bishophill Junior: street and building
16 St Mary Bishophill Junior: house
17 Fetter Lane: baths
18 Queen's Hotel (1–9 Micklegate) public buildings
19 37 Bishophill Senior: houses and terrace
20 St Mary Bishophill Senior: house
21 58–9 Skeldergate: street and well

Datum; this is 3.17m (10ft 3in) below the modern mean summer river level, and reflects how not only ground level but also river levels and sea levels have changed over the last 2000 years. Indeed, by the fourth century the wall had been demolished, and flood deposits overlay its remains – henceforth, floods were an intermittent threat.

Neither riverside wall nor flooding could dispel one newcomer to Britain – the black rat. Its recognition in Roman levels at York in the 1970s rewrote the history of the species, pushing its introduction

back by over 1000 years. Presumably it was a shipborne colonizer, entering on ships from across the Channel, and with its population periodically topped up by further new arrivals. Warm, wellbuilt Roman structures helped it to survive at the edge of its possible climatic range – but when Roman ships no longer came, and when (perhaps) the climate deteriorated in the post-Roman period, it died out, only to be reintroduced during more favourable conditions in the Viking Age.

Some of the water supply in the mid- to late second century was drawn from the Ouse in lead pipes, but at about the same time, elsewhere in the *colonia*, at Skeldergate, considerable effort and technical expertise went into making a 6m- (20ft) deep timber-lined well shaft, with a built-in filter bed of gravel to help purify the water (**56**).

Once major individual stone buildings were erected, they could continue in use for a long time. In the best example of this yet recognized, at Wellington Row, a later second-century rectangular stone building was soon rebuilt and extended after a fire; the floor level inside then rose throughout the third and early fourth century because successive floors consisted of layer upon layer of earth and/or cobbles. In the later fourth century and beyond up to 1m (3ft 3in) of dark silty loam built up. This type of deposit is found in later Roman contexts at many towns in Britain, and is often called 'dark earth'. It is interpreted here as a mixture of natural accumulation and rubbish dumping within the deserted and roofless shell of the building which, nevertheless, still stood 1–2m (3–6ft)

56 *View down a timber-lined well built* c. *AD 200 at Skeldergate. Scale 0.5m (19 1/2in).*

above the contemporary ground surface, and was finally covered with soil as late as the Anglo-Scandinavian period. Such long-term survival was not automatic, however. At 1–9 Micklegate a massive mid- to late third-century building, perhaps a bath-house, was demolished and levelled off by the end of the fourth century in a clear demonstration that land-use patterns were continuing to change and evolve at the very end of the Roman era (**57**).

It has to be admitted that knowledge of the environment of Anglian *Eoforwic* is patchy in the extreme. The excavations of 1985–6 at 46–54 Fishergate revealed timber buildings, but occupation had been nowhere near intensive enough to generate preservation of organic remains, and the average total depth of the deposits spanning nearly two centuries of occupation there was only about 0.1m (3in). Elsewhere, there have been very few sites where recognizably Anglian deposits or even undated sequences of layers which probably include such deposits have been excavated and where data about the environment has been recovered.

Within the fortress, the difficulties of dating layers which are situated between recognizably later fourth-century and recognizably late ninth/tenth-century deposits have already been noted. At 9 Blake Street an accumulation of grey/brown silty loams, averaging 0.3–0.4m (1ft–1ft 3in) in total depth, was discovered in what is interpreted as an open area; there was no sign of thick 'dark earth' deposits. South-east of the fortress, at 16–22 Coppergate, a 0.85m- (2ft 9in) deep, basically uniform build-up of light-grey-coloured loamy soil represented the fifth–ninth centuries, and no traces of any occupation – no signs of structures, hearths, pits, floor layers etc. – were recognized within it. Two different explanations can be advanced to account for the homogeneity of the build-up. One is that it represents a completely natural accumulation, consisting of wind-blown and water-borne silts combining with whatever may survive from the growth of a self-seeded plant cover. The other is that quantities of soil were brought from elsewhere to cover the rather infertile and intractable Roman deposits and to allow agriculture, or at

57 *Excavation assistants stand in holes for the upright posts of a timber building, apparently cut deliberately into the demolished and levelled wall of a large Roman building at 1–9 Micklegate.*

least the equivalent of allotments; ploughing, this argument goes, has churned up the imported soil and given it a uniform appearance. The question of which interpretation is correct remains unanswered at present. Its resolution is crucial because upon it hinge other major issues of interpretation. If the layers built up, undisturbed, where they are excavated, the Anglian pottery which is sometimes found in small quantities in them could well point to adjacent occupation/activity. If, however, dumping accounts for the soil build-up, then the pottery could have been brought along from elsewhere too.

The continuing use of various Roman street-lines such as Stonegate or Petergate through the Anglian period to the Viking Age and on to the present day is relatively certain, but determining which of the city's other streets may have originated at a particular time in the pre-Norman era is often difficult, if not impossible. The form and origin of some of the street names may give some guidance, although they must be considered carefully and not solely from a linguistic viewpoint – after all, both Stonegate and Petergate are streets of Roman origin whose names contain Old Norse elements. Nonetheless, Aldwark is an example of a name of Old English rather than Old Norse derivation, and it may therefore predate the arrival of Scandinavian Old Norse speakers.

Given the difficulties of recognizing streets which originated in the Anglian period, there is a temptation to take the large number of names with Old Norse elements at face value, and to suggest a great growth in the density of activity in the Viking Age. And indeed, wherever excavation has indicated when streets were created by identifying the origins of settlement alongside, the answer has consistently been that it was in the later ninth or tenth centuries. This was the case along the waterfront of the former *colonia* at 59 Skeldergate, and was seen even more dramatically outside the former fortress at 16–22 Coppergate. There, above the build-up of homogeneous soils attributed to the Anglian period, activity and occupation resumed in the later ninth century. By the early tenth century the layout of tenement plots had been created and single-storey post-and-wattle buildings had been erected at the street frontage. So much organic debris and refuse was being generated by this occupation that from *c.* 930 onwards it was accumulating at a faster rate than it was rotting away. Decay was inhibited because in these oxygen-free conditions the bacteria which usually attack organic and other materials cannot survive. This led to excellent organic preservation, and also resulted in a rapid raising of ground level by as much as 2cm (1 in) a year (**58**).

The remarkable preservation of timber, twigs, leaves, plants and other vegetation shows what was growing in and around *Jorvik*. Roots of elder bushes were found in position, and it is thought that nettles and docks also grew in some backyards. Many species of trees were harvested for wattlework – the favourites seem to have been hazel and willow, and oak was used for main stakes and posts. Study of samples of the interwoven wattlework rods used to make wall panels has suggested that the trees were deliberately coppiced – that is, there was a regular cycle of cutting off suitable rods, perhaps every 5–7 years.

Jorvik, like *Eoforwic* before it and much of medieval York later, was predominantly a timber town, but it was only the street frontages that were densely built up with houses/workshops. In the areas behind there was open space, albeit sometimes subdivided, which was used for several overlapping purposes. Some at least of the domestic and industrial rubbish could be disposed of there; it was where cesspits could be dug (no inside toilets nor recognizable chamber pots in the Anglian or Anglo-Scandinavian periods); there is some evidence that animals such as pigs and chickens could be kept there, rooting around among the debris; and perhaps this was also where, every now and again, a cow or sheep was brought in on the hoof, slaughtered and butchered.

The picture, then, is of backyards which had a rich and ripe mixture of animal dung, rotting plant matter and domestic rubbish on the surface. Into this unappealing compound were dug

58 *The south-east wall of the Roman fortress, seen below Parliament Street in 1976, with the medieval build-up of soil and debris which gradually submerged it visible on the right against the modern shoring. Scale: 1m (3ft 3in).*

cesspits which, in due course, were backfilled with more rubbish while others were dug nearby, perhaps even through the remains of ones in use a generation earlier. It is sometimes difficult to be certain of the primary purpose for which particular holes were dug. Many were designed for more than merely instant use; their carefully constructed wattlework linings prove that they were intended to remain open for some time. A few, lined with barrels, are most likely to have been wells, for they would have acted most efficiently as filters in the foul conditions. Nonetheless strong stomachs would have been necessary, and urban water is unlikely to have been a drink of choice in the Viking Age.

In order to help the occupants to keep a footing in the uneven and slippery backyards, mats or paths of wattlework were laid in places. Many of the smaller inhabitants of the area, however, could not avoid falling into open pits – a modern biologist wishing to design a method for capturing a sample of the rodents, amphibians and other tiny creatures frequenting the site could hardly have come up with a better system of traps. The animal skeletons recovered from the Coppergate pits show that house mice, black rats and frogs were common throughout the Viking Age; their numbers were obviously not kept down by the dogs and cats which also prowled around, or by aerial hunters such as red kites or buzzards. At the start of the Viking Age shrews, voles and wood mice were also relatively common, but the increasingly intensive occupation seems rapidly to have driven them out.

One subtle index of the growth in pollution as the Viking Age progressed comes from a study of the fish species which are represented by their bones. In the very earliest Viking Age levels, in the later ninth and the early tenth centuries, species such as grayling, barbel and shad, which can tolerate only the cleanest of water, were present. By the mid to late tenth century, however, they had disappeared, presumably because the waters had been muddied (or worse).

The margins of the Ouse, at least, were certainly altered during the Viking Age. Excavations at North Street revealed how successive wattlework revetments were inserted at the water's edge. These operations were episodes in what was to be a continuous if intermittent campaign throughout the medieval period to utilize the riverside to best effect. Perhaps the single most dramatic change along the waterfront, however, was the creation of a new, sole bridging point at the spot where the present Ouse Bridge stands. A bridge here is first mentioned in a document referring to 1154, but its origination has long been assumed to go back to the Viking Age. There are two reasons for this. One, the fact that the streets at either end have Old Norse names, is not a particularly reliable guide, for elsewhere the Old Norse element *gata* is found in the street name Newgate, which was first recorded in 1328. A second, more convincing reason has become increasingly apparent since about 1970, and is the fact that the area around and beyond the northern end of the bridge was an important sector of *Jorvik*, which was partly laid out in the early tenth century.

The reason why and the precise date when the bridge was moved downstream for 250m (775ft) from its Roman position are not clear, and it is possible that for a time the only means of crossing were either ford or ferry. Whenever the new bridge was erected, it may have simply been the importance of the burgeoning area on the northern bank, south-east of the old fortress, which acted like a magnet for its builders. Another contributory factor may well have been the topography of the new approaches: mapping of the underlying natural strata has recently demonstrated that there was a natural spur narrowing the width of the river just here. However, another insight into conditions at the river margins can be gained from some of the city's street names. King Street, just downstream from Ouse Bridge, was known as *Kergathe c.* 1200, a name which is derived from the Old Norse *kiarr* through the Middle English *ker* and means 'marsh' or 'wet ground'. On the opposite south bank, it has been suggested that the street name Skeldergate means Shelf Street, implying that there was a recognizable ledge or terrace here in the Viking Age.

Although the Norman Conquest brought considerable change to the appearance of individual buildings such as the Minster, there is no sign of any great change in overall living conditions. What affected most citizens for the longest time was the creation of two new defended enclaves, each of which contained a motte and bailey castle. 'Domesday Book' records the bare statistic that one of the city's seven 'shires' was *vastata in castellis* (destroyed for the castles), but the areas which the Normans razed to the ground are only partly obvious today. To the south-west of the Ouse only the motte called Baile Hill is recognizable; the bailey (courtyard) area beyond was still discernible into the mid-nineteenth century, but is now full of Victorian terraced houses. Across the river, York Castle seems a much more complete and coherent entity, even though there is not much of the medieval fabric left apart from the eleventh- and twelfth-century motte, crowned with the mid-thirteenth-century Clifford's Tower, and some of the curtain wall incorporating the drawbridge pit outside a now blocked gate. Yet excavations in 1981 behind Tower Street, where a hotel now stands, showed that originally the castle covered a larger area, for unexpectedly an outer ditch was located, defending a previously unknown outer bailey (**59**).

Another major component of William the Conqueror's impact on York was designed to give the castle greater protection. The River Foss was dammed, inundating low-lying areas immediately upstream and creating a pool of sluggish water called *stagnum regis*, 'the King's fish pool'. The immediate responses of the owners of properties bordering the King's Pool are uncertain, for it is impossible to date some potentially relevant archaeological discoveries sufficiently accurately. Excavations in Piccadilly, just west of the present course of the Foss, revealed part of a wickerwork revetment which is interpreted as an attempt to define the river's edge; it seems to be mid-eleventh-century, but can't be placed securely on one or other side of the Norman Conquest. Further upstream, in Hungate, excavation in 1950–1 exposed what seems to be a riverside embankment. The appearance of the Pool certainly provides an obvious context for the creation of this feature, but the dating evidence is not sufficiently precise to confirm a definite link.

Several excavations along Piccadilly have failed to reveal any evidence for silting of the Pool in the late eleventh–thirteenth centuries. This meshes well with historical records that fish were kept in the Pool for sale, which implies both clear water and careful maintenance. Silts associated with pottery dated to the fourteenth–sixteenth centuries have, however, been recognized. Freshwater mussels indicate that this silting occurred in relatively clean conditions, and hardly any rubbish was found in these layers. Here, archaeology and documentary records seem to diverge, for a succession of reports from the fourteenth century onwards condemn the build up of sewage, filth and silt in the Pool.

Although passage from the Foss to the Ouse was barred by William the Conqueror's dam, there is both historical and archaeological evidence for activity along the Foss's banks. About 200m (220 yds) above the dam, at 50 Piccadilly, a series of waterside dumps which included much domestic and organic debris was laid down in the fourteenth century. They were succeeded by a substantial timber revetment, consisting of a row of vertical posts, 0.3–0.4m (1ft–1ft 3in) apart, supported and reinforced on their landward side by a second row of posts, raked at an angle (**60**). More horizontal timbers and wattlework on the landward side served to consolidate and support the area further. In the fifteenth century there was another attempt to revet the riverbank, and later dumps of soil and debris showed that from then until the twentieth century there were virtually continuous efforts to raise ground levels hereabouts.

Upstream, by *c.* 1270, was *Peseholm*, now Peasholme Green, 'the islet or low-lying area where peas grow'; a century earlier, in the same area between Saviourgate and the Foss, there is a reference to a Marsh Street. Although the Pool existed until the eighteenth century, when the Foss was canalized, successive town plans show

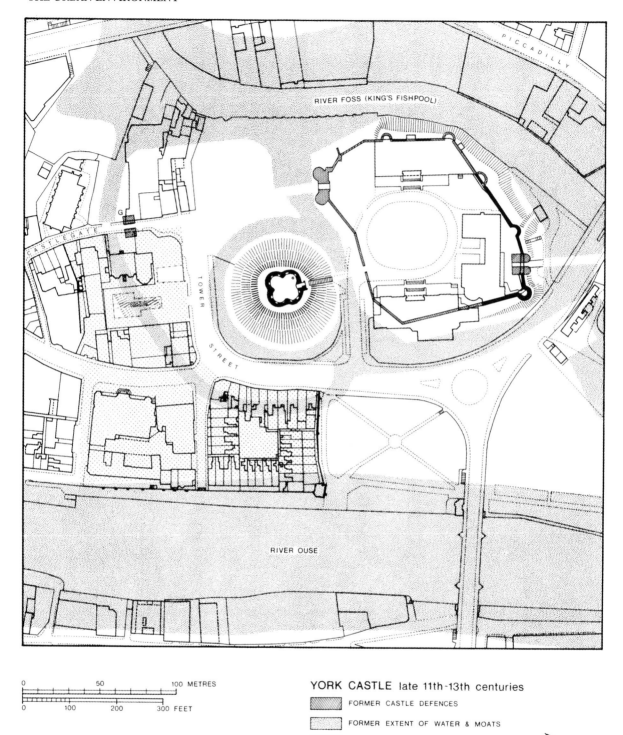

59 *York Castle in the late eleventh–thirteenth centuries, showing possible lines for the newly located outer ditch and the water defences.*

60 *Recording the fourteenth-century timber revetment to the River Foss at 50 Piccadilly.*

its size shrinking in the sixteenth century and later; the name Foss Islands Road is another testimony to its reclamation. As a postscript to the Pool, there is evidence that its condition contributed to a distinctive local beverage. Near the castle, reported Thomas Baskerville in 1677, 'dead standing water . . . corrupts the air, of which they make a strong, heavy, sluggish ale . . . I could not well digest it.'

While the Foss was really a backwater during the Middle Ages, the Ouse was a hive of commercial activity (p. 92), but there have been few opportunities to get archaeological evidence for the Norman riverfront hereabouts, although a form of box revetment construction to stabilize eleventh-century dumping was seen in the 1993 North Street excavation on the south bank. On the north bank a substantial stone wall of the late twelfth or early thirteenth century, seen in a short isolated length at 39–41 Coney Street, may represent a riverside wall or, more probably, part of a riverside building. It stood on the lip of a steep drop towards the river, but some 25m (80ft) inland from the present riverfront.

Downstream of Ouse Bridge, the riverside has been investigated in several small-scale excavations on the south bank, along Skeldergate. Here

archaeology confirms and amplifies such written records as a petition to the King by local residents, who objected to the damage to their properties by water surges deflected from the north bank by riverside reclamation there undertaken by the Franciscan friars. In 1305 these residents were given royal permission to consolidate their own river frontages.

Excavation in Skeldergate has revealed that *c.* 1200 water-borne alluvium came to within 3m (10ft) of the modern street line; successive reclamations extended the properties here by a total of about 28m (90ft) into the former river. The most substantial gains were made in the fifteenth century, when the erection of a double line of limestone walls, parallel to the river, reclaimed 20m (65ft) of river's edge. On the landward side a flight of steps led down to an arched opening through the inner wall (**61**), which gave access to a vaulted passage leading to the outer wall and the newly established riverside. Goods could

61 *Steps down to a blocked fifteenth-century watergate at Skeldergate.*

62 *Watergates, one open and one blocked up, in the later sixteenth-century river wall on the north-east bank of the Ouse, behind Coney Street.*

presumably be offloaded into the passageway, while other occupation or activity took place on the reclaimed land and, indeed, above the vault. Just downstream was the Common Crane, first recorded in the fifteenth century, where all non-resident merchants had to offload their goods and pay appropriate tolls to the city.

As the river was increasingly constricted into a narrower channel, the banks became ever more vulnerable to flooding, particularly when either melt-water from snowfalls or an unusually great volume of rainwater swelled the flow. Flooding was a natural hazard of the river – others were man-made. For example, sewage was emptied directly from *novae latrinae, Anglice, les New Pryves* ('the new latrines, [called] in English, the new privies') which were built in 1367 in an arch of Ouse Bridge, below the *maison dieu* (almshouse)

there. There is, however, no precise measure of the degree of pollution in the river, or the extent of its effect on the environment downstream. It certainly did not wipe out all the fish stock: in 1376, two Austin friars from the Lendal friary were drowned in the Ouse when their boat was capsized by fish-garths, post-and-wattle fish-traps which were positioned across the river.

The last major reclamation on the north bank of the Ouse and upstream of Ouse Bridge took place in the sixteenth century, judging by the single excavation which has investigated it. Today limestone riverside walls extend virtually all the way from the Guildhall to Ouse Bridge, punctuated at intervals by quite tall and narrow arched openings (mostly now blocked up) at river level (**62**). Excavations in 1974 at 39–41 Coney Street showed that the opening there led into a stone-lined passageway, built *c.* 1575. In some ways it is similar to that built a century or so earlier in Skeldergate; it served as access to the river, and perhaps also provided a place where small craft could be beached. By *c.* 1700, however, it was redundant, and the passage was backfilled with rubble and debris; the Skeldergate example had suffered a similar fate about 100 years before.

If the waterfront was changing, the river itself was still a convenient sewer. In the sixteenth and seventeenth centuries the riverbank downstream from Ouse Bridge was the site of the 'Pudding Holes', a public washing-place not only for clothes but also for the innards of animals, used for making black puddings. Contemporary exhortations and bye-laws about rubbish dumping in the river suggest foul, unhygienic conditions. Thus it is not surprising that when, in 1616, there was a first, ultimately unsuccessful, attempt to draw water from the Ouse and to distribute it throughout the city by a series of pipes, the extraction point chosen was at the upstream boundary of the city's defences, at Lendal Tower. A new beginning was made in 1677, and the Tower continued to hold machinery for the waterworks until 1836; it is still the headquarters of The York Waterworks PLC.

In the eighteenth century, with the emphasis on York's social importance, a New Walk with trees and plants was laid out beside the river in 1732, for the enjoyment of the gentry. In 1757 a lock was built at Naburn, 8km (5 miles) downstream, in order to raise the water-level sufficiently to ease the passage of boats. Within a century, however, water transport was to suffer major competition from the railways; today, only newsprint is commercially freighted to York by water (**colour plate 15**).

Changes to the urban environment came slowly, imperceptibly, as the medieval period progressed. The practice of building some houses in stone was adopted in the Norman period, and this would have resulted in correspondingly less wood and wattle debris accumulating. This, however, seems to have been only a temporary and occasional blip in the pattern of York's building; there is both documentary and archaeological evidence for Norman stone buildings being demolished in the thirteenth/fourteenth centuries

and replaced with timber-framed structures.

A much more long-lasting and therefore important change came with the pragmatic decision to adopt tile roofing instead of thatch. Finds of tile fragments in excavations suggest that this was happening in York from the twelfth century onwards, although the speed at which thatch was banished can't yet be gauged. At first the roof tiles were of Roman form, laid side by side on the roof with the gaps between covered by bridging tiles of semi-circular cross-section, but by the thirteenth century plain flat pegged or ribbed tiles, each laid to overlap its neighbour, had become standard.

The reduction in thatch was probably a major factor in lessening the amount of organic debris generated by the medieval town. A second factor was the trend towards timber-framed buildings, more strongly built than some of their post-and-wattle predecessors. This, combined with the practice of erecting these buildings on stone footings or foundations which protected the upright posts from rotting in the ground, further prolonged the life of buildings (**63**). Another significant move was that towards substituting brick or tile infilling for wattlework panels between the main timber elements. This too cut down the need for replacement and repair, and thus minimized the quantity of organic debris. An increased incidence of either timber-boarded or tiled floors within houses also contributed to this trend.

A third important factor in altering the urban environment through reducing organic debris was the increasing density of occupation on tenement plots. In the pre-Norman period occupation had been focused on the street frontage, but by the thirteenth century, with the growth in population and industrial output, what had been open backyards had become increasingly built up. There was now less room to dispose of domestic rubbish and industrial debris, and also less room for other important requirements such as wells and cesspits. The result seems to have been that more urban waste had to be disposed of outside the tenement plots. There was also a move away from outdoor cesspits (**64**) to built-in, or at least

63 *Below- and above-ground archaeology in Walmgate: excavating house foundations approximately contemporary with the* c. *1400 Bowes Morrell House across the road.*

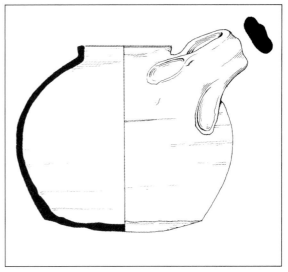

64 *Twelfth-century toilet seat and cesspit at 16–22 Coppergate. Scale: 0.2m. (8in).*

65 *Late medieval pottery urinal from Bedern. Scale: 1:4.*

purpose-built, garderobes, whence the residues could periodically be dug out and carted away; this too cut down on the build-up of organic waste.

The later medieval period saw another change in matters lavatorial with the introduction of the purpose-made urinal (**65**). Groups of small jugs found in cesspits at Bedern (**66**) suggest that common types of pottery vessels frequently relieved the need for a specialized vessel; white salts encrusted inside a similar jug found at Aldwark in 1976 are evidence that it, at least, ended its life as a urinal. Recognizable chamber pots, by contrast, are not found earlier than the sixteenth/seventeenth centuries, but there is historical evidence that, as with urinals, more common forms of pottery vessels such as standard cooking pots served the purpose in earlier centuries. Thus the appearance of 'sanitary wares' in the archaeological record doesn't necessarily indicate changes in habits or hygiene.

The result of all these various changes, so far as the archaeologist in York is concerned, is that the later in the medieval period you are digging, the less the organic component in the soil. As a knock-on effect, whatever organic artefacts were in use are less likely to survive. So from about the fourteenth century onwards the archaeological data

available are only a fraction of those for, say, the tenth–twelfth centuries. The layers themselves are generally thinner in the later medieval period, for without the organic constituents only the mineral component survives. Thus time is compressed in the archaeological stratification. A given thickness of layers close to the surface, where they are most vulnerable to modern disturbance or destruction, may represent several hundred years of occupation and activity, whereas lower down in the sequence a similar bulk of earlier deposits might represent decades rather than centuries.

66 *Fourteenth-century brick-lined cesspit at Bedern, with a jug urinal at the base. Scale: 0.2m (8in).*

Whatever the archaeologist might think about conditions improving in the fourteenth and later centuries, the judgment of contemporaries is telling. Edward III, for one, was not impressed by York, commenting in 1332 on 'the abominable smell abounding in the said city more than in any other city of the realm from dung and manure, and other filth and dirt wherewith the streets and lanes are filled and obstructed'. With animals of all sorts driven along on the way to market, and ox-carts and horses providing transport, the royal displeasure is partly explicable, although why it should have been worse in York than in other comparable towns isn't clear. The state of medieval streets is lost to archaeology, for they are nearly always inaccessible beneath their modern, widened, successors. The very fact that Stonegate (first mentioned in 1148–75) and Pavement (1329) are the only two names which imply a good road surface suggests that most streets were in a worse condition.

The contrast between pleasant and unpleasant aspects of medieval life is neatly summed up in the College of Vicars Choral (p. 110). Their gardens contained a variety of vegetables and herbs, there was a walled orchard, and they even cultivated a small vineyard. Yet one of their common wells was described as being sited 'near the dunghill south-west of the Hall'.

Medieval access to a water supply was most usually gained by digging a well within the property's backyard. Many were lined with barrels, which originally probably contained wine or some other drink; they could be stacked one above another in order to reach the depth of the water table. If preservative conditions are good, even the willow withy bindings of the hazel withy rings around the barrel staves can survive (**67**). Alternatively a square shaft could be supported with a purpose-built wooden lining of one sort or another, while in the later medieval period brick-lined or even stone-lined shafts became more common. The lining itself acted as something of a filter, but only a sixteenth-century stone-lined well excavated at Coppergate was designed to incorporate a deliberate filtration mechanism at the base. Wells were presumably abandoned when their linings gave way and water quality dropped. They were then infilled with whatever debris was to hand.

When rebuilding began after the Civil War, fire damage to timber-framed buildings caused

67 *a) Fourteenth-century barrel-well at 16–22 Coppergate, with iron-bound wooden bucket and chain at its bottom. Scale 0.2m (8in).*

b) Some barrel staves removed to show their outer binding. Scale: 1m (3ft 3in).

the Corporation to decree that new construction work should be in brick. At least one late seventeenth-century visitor, Thomas Baskerville, thought that a greater conflagration was required for York's good: 'in general the whole town is old timber buildings and must have a purgation by fire if ever it arise in beauty like Northampton or London'. His hope was not fulfilled; instead it has been piecemeal losses which have thinned the timber-framed buildings.

In the sixteenth–eighteenth centuries there were still relatively large areas of open ground within the city, contrasting with the dense occupation which characterized most of the areas which were built up. Only Dean's Park now remains – south of the Ouse the Victorian era saw the first railway station take over one such area, and terraces of housing infill the others. And, in the twentieth century, we have seen an end of the 'slaughter houses, dung-heaps, pig-sties, etc., which unfortunately subsist in the heart of the town', as a nineteenth-century commentator wrote, and upgraded a water supply which in the last century was described as 'so turbid and dirty as scarcely to be fit for washing, and still less for cooking or being drunk'.

5
Earning a living

The ways in which York's citizens have made their living have varied considerably over the centuries, largely in response to their contemporary social framework. The Iron Age Celtic Britons of the Northumbrian countryside were mostly full-time farmers. There were some specialist craftsmen, for example metalworkers, attached to the retinues of aristocrats, but there was no cash or market economy, and relatively few goods in circulation other than those made at home by domestic production for domestic consumption.

In contrast, the arrival of the Roman army and the foundation of *Eboracum* necessitated not only the feeding of the 5000 legionaries but also the supply of all their requirements. They brought with them some gear that had already seen service for many years – some instantly recognizable pottery types, for example, made in France – but such stuff was continuously in need of re-supply. Initially food supplies were secured, in part at least, by importing grain from the south of England or even, perhaps, from France. Traces of the foundations of two superimposed timber buildings which were found close to the River Ouse, below W. H. Smith's shop at 39–41 Coney Street, are interpreted as representing warehouses which can be dated to the later first and early second century (see **16**). Grain or grain beetles provided clear evidence for at least some of their contents; they were a transit point through which water-borne supplies reached the fortress. Whether this represents a purely military operation, or if private

commercial dealers had a hand in it, is unclear. By *c.* 150, however, these warehouses were militarily redundant, demolished and covered by a new roadway; local grain supplies had probably become available, again perhaps to the profit of local landowners.

This very basic aspect of what was a 'command' economy can also and more obviously be seen in some other facets of military supply. A standard range of pottery vessels, for example, was made by military potters, apparently using a military manual which defined the required shapes and sizes. Military potting seems to have taken place from *Eboracum*'s founding until the mid-third century; a zone off the east corner of the fortress, in the Aldwark-Peasholme Green area, certainly held some military tile kilns and probably pottery kilns as well. Stacks of tiles were found at St Cuthbert's churchyard, Peasholme Green, in 1836 and again in 1911, the York Excavation Group has recovered a lot of pottery kiln waste from the gardens of the Borthwick Institute next door, and more has been found nearby in Aldwark and in Peasholme Green. This vicinity, quite close to the river Foss and sited on alluvial clay, a good potter's clay, was ideal for ceramic production. Yet by the mid-third century the industry here was wound up; the last phase of military production was that which included the production of the head pots (see p. 52). From the early second century onwards, some legionary veterans had been producing military-style wares at a site about 3km (2 miles) north-east of the fortress, and local or regional suppliers were to be increasingly important in the last two centuries of Roman occupation.

As well as these local suppliers there was importation of foreign pottery. High-quality tablewares, notably the red, shiny, so-called Samian pottery, came from France in bulk – the broken debris from a central store of the 70s was found on the site of the Stonegate Arcade at 9 Blake Street. Finely made drinking beakers and other pots were brought to *Eboracum* from the Rhineland; it may have been the profits from this business that enabled the French-born merchant Lucius Viducius Placidus to erect a dedicatory arch and passage in *Eboracum* in AD 221 (see **43**). Other imported pottery vessels included the varied types of *amphora*, the containers of their day, which were brought to the city for their contents rather than for themselves. Olive oil from southern Spain and North Africa, wine from southern France, north-eastern Spain, Italy, Rhodes and Egypt, fish products from Spain and fruits from Palestine all involved producers, middlemen, shippers, agents and distributors. Other than the *amphorae*, the traces of this network found at *Eboracum* amount to the stone pillars which supported the raised floor of a riverside warehouse on the civilian side of the Ouse.

Other military requirements included metals from which to manufacture weaponry, tools, utensils, etc. The military workshops for this activity remain elusive, but a substantial group of metalwork debris, including slag from both iron- and copperworking, iron offcuts and iron tools has been found in the *colonia* at Tanner Row. Despite its location, this material, which dates to the later second century, may represent military rather than civilian craftsmanship and demand. The tombstone of a smith, showing him at his anvil wielding hammer and tongs, demonstrates that successful craftsmen could prosper. There is also unusual evidence for glassworking, found within the military workshop area in excavation at Coppergate; everyday pottery jars had been used to hold the molten glass, which had cooled and solidified in the base of the pots. Another

rare body of evidence is that for leatherworking. The legion required tents, belts, bridles, shoes and much else besides, but normally both finished products and manufacturing debris, being organic materials, rapidly rot away. In parts of York where the soil is moist, however, they can survive, and a remarkable collection has been discovered in the *colonia* at Tanner Row. It includes waste offcut pieces and large numbers of shoe fragments, as well as pieces of army tents.

As a final example of Roman industry, again one that had both military and civilian connections, there is the quarrying and supply of building stone. In time all of the fortress buildings were built with stone, and the walls and gates required yet more. Finely cut blocks of limestone and larger blocks of millstone grit were used both in the fortress and later in the *colonia*; sandstone slabs were used sometimes for roofing, instead of tiles, and at least some roads were paved with stone or stone chippings, although elsewhere river cobbles were used. While some of the stone working was presumably undertaken either by soldiers or under military requisition, particularly in the earlier centuries of Roman rule, it is likely that private enterprise accounted for some of the trade later on in the era.

As a provincial capital, there would inevitably have been a bureaucracy at work in *Eboracum* with adminstrators, tax inspectors, lawyers etc. and their back-up secretariat. There is little evidence that *Eboracum* was a manufacturing centre, but the *colonia* does seem to have been a social centre. The main evidence for this comes from the nature of the buildings which have been discovered, albeit intermittently, over the centuries. They include several that can be interpreted as fine-quality town houses, with spacious rooms enhanced with mosaic floors and painted walls. Others seem to be public buildings; a late third-century structure tantalizingly revealed at 9 Micklegate, for example, can be interpreted as an impressive public bath-house. The dedications and temples of the civilian town, mainly known through the records of nineteenth-century discoveries, also suggest that this was a place where

Romanized native landowners, successful entrepreneurs and the Roman governmental élite mingled socially, enjoyed themselves and displayed their status. A wide range of service industries presumably supplied their requirements, but this would not have been a very large-scale source of employment, for the *colonia's* total population probably numbered only a few thousand.

There is no evidence for craft, manufacturing or trading activities at York in the fifth–sixth centuries. When evidence does appear again, dated to the seventh century, it has three components. Firstly, there is that which is connected to the presence of the Church. There is as yet no sign of the works of the stonemasons and glassworkers who were brought to York first by Paulinus and then by Wilfrid, but the gravemarkers from the late seventh–eighth centuries found at York Minster indicate that a school of stonecarvers had been established under ecclesiastical patronage in *Eoforwic* (**68**).

Secondly, there is the evidence for foreign contacts that has gradually been pieced together through the recognition of imported pottery vessels and other items. The pottery sherds were found in small numbers on many of the usually small-scale waterfront excavations of the 1970s, 80s and 90s. They are characteristically wheel-thrown table vessels, made in what are now northern France, Belgium and Holland in the eighth and ninth centuries. They are of better quality and more attractive than the locally produced pottery, and could have been traded for themselves, but it is equally, if not more, probable that they were simply the personal possessions of foreign merchants who brought other items including wine and lava quernstones to *Eoforwic*.

Thirdly, there is evidence for a range of craft and manufacturing, found in excavation at 46–54 Fishergate, just downstream of the confluence of the Foss and the Ouse. The site, which was not densely occupied, produced debris from ironworking, non-ferrous metalworking (including gold, silver, lead-alloy and copper-alloys), bone- and antler-working, woodworking, leatherworking,

textile-making and glassworking. The difficulty comes when trying to establish what exactly these data tell us about the way in which manufacturing production was organized in the Anglian town. Neither the quantity nor the localized distribution of any particular type of item on the site was sufficient to point to specific production areas. Indeed, there is no proof that large-scale and specialized production took place here, although there may be good reasons for the paucity of evidence – some debris might have been tipped into the nearby river rather than disposed of on site and some may have been recycled (the metal or the glass, for example).

Although a series of coins found on the site, including both local Northumbrian and continental issues, suggests that commerce was conducted hereabouts, and despite the presence of some imported pottery and a handful of other foreign goods, it could be argued that production was only on a domestic scale and was not geared to a vibrant, competitive market economy. Indeed, there is complementary evidence from the animal bone debris which suggests, through its uniformity, that a centralized power, not market forces, was supplying the settlement with meat.

The currently accepted explanation for all this is that manufacturing and trade in *Eoforwic* were established and carefully regulated by the Northumbrian kings for their own benefit. By assuring themselves of control of luxury items they could use them diplomatically to win the support of their own aristocracy and to demonstrate their own prestige. Therefore, craftsmen worked with raw materials supplied by the king, in a sector of the city set aside by the king, to produce goods which the king required, and to engage in trade with foreign merchants on the king's behalf. This was a pattern not confined to Northumbria; remains of broadly similar archaeological sites have been found in the other major Anglo-Saxon kingdoms. These sites are termed *wics* because that element appears in each of their contemporary place-names – *Lundenwic* (London) in the kingdom of Mercia, *Hamwic* (Southampton) in the kingdom of Wessex, *Gipeswic* (Ipswich) in

East Anglia, and Fordwich (Canterbury) in Kent.

In spite of the important breakthrough made in the discovery of the Fishergate site, *Eoforwic* remains archaeologically indistinct. It's unclear how many people were working in the *wic* area; the Fishergate site is just a part of that zone, but whether it's the focus or on the periphery, whether or not it's representative, and whether the zone extends continuously for some way along the banks of the Foss and Ouse, or was a wholly separate entity, are still to be discovered.

Equally nebulous is our understanding of what exactly the foreign merchants took away from York in return for the goods they had brought. The range of items made at Fishergate was common to north-western Europe, and would not have commanded the attention of international merchants. Were the merchants paid in cash or

68 *Inhabited vinescroll on a cross-shaft* c. *700–800 from York Minster. Height: 28cm (11in).*

were there archaeologically invisible exports such as cloth? Solving these mysteries is what will eventually enable a clearer picture to emerge of the occupations of *Eoforwic's* inhabitants in the seventh–mid-ninth centuries. At present, however, it looks as if elements in the production of goods during this era may have been effected through another version of the 'command economy' already seen in Roman *Eboracum*.

If this is true, it all changed during the Anglo-Scandinavian period. The overwhelming majority of the Anglo-Scandinavian population were farmers or farm workers, owning, managing or labouring on estates and farms to produce food for themselves and/or a surplus for their landlords. Some of those who lived in *Jorvik* probably augmented their income by cultivating lands on the edge of the city, although the locations and sizes of these putative holdings are a matter of speculation.

But *Jorvik* was different from *Eoforwic* in terms both of the quantity, quality and variety of the goods which were made there. In the archaeological record which has been accumulated since the 1970s it has been possible to recognize, for the first time, what no other sources of information can provide – evidence that specialist craftsmen were producing everyday items on such a scale that they could have made a viable livelihood for themselves in the process. Indeed, the few parts of *Jorvik* which have been excavated show that from the early tenth century the Viking Age city was organized in a new and different way, with regular, long and narrow tenement plots defined so as to squeeze the maximum number of houses/workshops into the available space.

In this new setting worked craftsmen with a wide range of skills. Potters based somewhere in York or its environs now mass-produced a standardized range of wheel-thrown domestic wares which were technically superior to the hand-made/home-made pots of the previous era. Other craftsmen, like those at Coppergate, who made both iron objects and also worked gold, silver, copper alloys and lead alloys, were masters of a particular set of skills such as working raw materials at high temperature which enabled them to span a range of related technical processes. It may be more than coincidence that the making of glass with a high lead content was also undertaken in this part of Coppergate in this era. Leatherworking, including both the making and mending of shoes, was another trade widely practised in this part of the Viking Age town; large quantities of leather offcuts have been found at several sites in Coppergate and Pavement, and cobblers' lasts have been found below Lloyds Bank at 6–8 Pavement.

It is possible, judging by the archaeological evidence, that it was the trades predominating in some streets during the Viking Age which gave those streets the names by which they are still known today. Coppergate is the clearest example: the 'gate' element, common in York, comes from the Old Norse word *gata* meaning 'street', while the 'Copper' element is also from an Old Norse word *koppari*, meaning 'cupmaker'. Ample evidence for the cupmaking process, in which blocks of wood were hollowed out on a lathe, was recovered in the excavation at 16–22 Coppergate – waste wood, some finished but damaged products, and parts of the turner's toolkit (**69**). Given that the wooden debris and rejects would be useful firewood, the amount of turners' waste which remained to be discovered can certainly be interpreted as representing wood-turning on a commercial rather than a domestic scale.

There is evidence for other manufacturing activities too, but on a smaller scale. Bone and antler were important raw materials, used for both very simple as well as quite sophisticated objects. At the basic end of the scale, virtually anyone with a knife could whittle out a bone pin, or make a simple whistle from a bird's leg bone, and such things were doubtless home-made. Composite antler combs, on the other hand, required not only the collection of material but knowledge of how best to cut it, so as to counteract the stresses of matted tresses. The high quality of the finished articles speaks of professionalism, although the dispersed incidence and relatively low quantities of comb-making debris suggest intermittent production which may have been on a seasonal basis, or by itinerant comb-makers, or indeed both.

Jet and amber, two soft rocks which can be cut to shape, bored through, ground and polished with relative ease, were both crafted in *Jorvik*, although here again the debris generated has been found in fairly small quantities, albeit on several sites. This may suggest cottage-industry status – occasional working for commercial purposes, but as a supplement to other forms of livelihood rather than as a mainstay of survival. The same may be true for much of the textile

69 *A tenth-century wood-turner at Coppergate* (Chris Evans).

production, evidence for which, particularly in the forms of spindle whorls, bone needles and other tools, has been found quite ubiquitously. It is difficult to gauge the scale of production from this equipment, but even the presence of dyestuffs at the Coppergate site is not a sufficient reason to require that textile making there was on a professional basis; both the technology and the raw materials of dying were, after all, quite simply and readily available.

One aspect of the textiles found at Coppergate could, however, suggest a professional approach – the unusual collection of over 20 silk fragments. They represent importation, in this instance probably from Byzantium (Istanbul), and it looks as if a Coppergate resident specialized in turning the silk cloth into saleable objects such as head-scarves. This too might well have been a very occasional occupation, not at all a full-time job. Yet it did require either the services of middlemen or direct access to whoever transported the cloth. This introduces another category of inhabitant of Viking Age York, the international dealer. By no means every foreign object found in *Jorvik* represents overseas trade, and indeed the evidence for some of the precise geographical areas of contact, although exotic and beguiling, consists of only a single object which may have been passed from hand to hand along a considerable chain of mercantile or personal links. Viewed in this light, some of the branch-lines of contact such as the Red Sea area, which is represented by a solitary cowrie shell, can be seen as peripherals to a main shipment route which brought goods such as silk from the eastern end of the Mediterranean. This was one route along which, at least in the tenth century, goods were brought to *Jorvik*; a second was across the English Channel from northern France, Germany and the Low Countries whence, as in the previous era, came wines and lava quernstones; a third was via the North Sea from Scandinavia, particularly from Denmark and Norway and the Norse settlements of Orkney and Shetland, which between them supplied sharpening stones, soapstone cooking vessels, and dyestuffs; and a fourth route was across the Irish Sea from Dublin and other Hiberno-Scandinavian towns.

Among the occupations practised in Viking Age York there were others that are easily overlooked. Building, and the supply of raw materials for building, must have occupied many man-hours. The city was essentially a timber town, with most structures made from wood and/or interwoven wattlework rods, with thatch for roofs. This material had to be collected; perhaps harvested would be a more accurate description, as there is some evidence for deliberate, not random, choice of materials. The stuff came, presumably, from the city's immediate hinterland. Was it brought on an *ad hoc* basis, supplied from their rural estates by landlords with holdings in both town and countryside, to accomplish building projects on their urban properties; or was there an open timber market? In the small sample of *Jorvik's* buildings that has been excavated there are some striking indications of uniformity in construction. Is this because there were also specialist builders, or does it again reflect the influence of a particular individual, who could dictate to his own workforce what he wanted them to build on adjacent plots? A final question over the building business concerns the supply of stone for the few but prestigious buildings that were built to last. Churches are the only ones yet discovered, but the cathedral, perhaps the palaces of the king, the archbishop and the earl, and possibly parts of the defences, such as the gateways, may also have been stone-built. In the instances recovered to date, the stonework has been reused Roman material, obtained by dismantling either standing or buried parts of Roman buildings. Technically difficult pieces such as archways were particularly prized. One example, in the Viking Age church at Kirk Hammerton, 13.5km (8½ miles) from York, is wholly Roman in workmanship, and has been brought from its original site, probably in York, for recycling. Is this the reverse of the rural estate–urban property relationship suggested previously; or was there a consistent and specialized crew of stone providers, supplying an open market for monumental masonry?

The feeding of so big a population as *Jorvik's* – in the order of perhaps 15,000 people – itself offered opportunities for earning a living. The mention of the street name Shambles (in its Latin form, *in macellis*) in 1086 in 'Domesday Book', suggests that there were already specialist butchers in the earlier eleventh-century city. Much of the diet was presumably brought to markets in *Jorvik* by surrounding farmers, and some of the townsfolk probably augmented their purchases of foodstuffs with whatever they could grow on their own account. There may have been commercial fishermen plying a trade; the quantities of sea fish, oysters and mussels which have been recovered all point to at least semi-professional activity.

After the Norman Conquest, the Viking Age pattern and range of industries was continued, but with an increasing tendency towards specialization and towards the organization and regulation of crafts by guilds. In York there was a guild of leatherworkers by 1181, and a butchers' fraternity in the late thirteenth century; the earliest recorded craft regulations are those of the girdlers (makers of belts/belt fittings) dated 1307. There was at maximum something like 80 guilds in medieval York. Some, like the Bowyers, faded away in time as their craft became obsolete, but others such as the Taylors continue to this day. Now called the Merchant Taylors, they are the only craft guild to maintain an original guildhall, which dates from the late fourteenth century, although externally much altered in the seventeenth century.

Other industries or crafts have streets named after them – Bakehouse Lane (1312) and Cook Row (1340), although archaeological evidence is confined to a sixteenth- to seventeenth-century bakery above an earlier foundry at the Bedern (**colour plate 13**); Barker Row, alias Tanner Row, first recorded in 1524 (although the only, slightly later, archaeological evidence for this smelly trade comes from nearer the edge of town, in Walmgate); Fishergate (1070–88); Girdlergate (1360) replacing Glovergail (Glovemakers' Lane), a name current *c.* 1250–1315; Colliergate

(1303–4), the street of the charcoal dealers; Fetter Lane (1280) where felt-makers worked; Spurriergate (1538) recalling the spur-makers; Hosier Lane (1373) occupied by makers of woollen socks/stockings; Sadler Lane (1541); Haymongergate (1240) alias Nedlergate (1394), named from the needle-makers. The equation of Hornpot Lane (1295) with the craft of making objects such as drinking horns, spoons and window panes from horn was proved in Peter Wenham's excavations there in 1957–8. He found a pit in which the horns could be soaked to separate each from its bony core; the remains of nearly 500 such cores, mainly of oxen and goats, were found within it. There were also four small furnaces which could have heated the horns to make them easy to shape. These remains were dated to the fourteenth century; horners continued to work in York until the last hornworks closed in 1931.

York was an important centre for the manufacture of church furnishings, and fittings of many kinds which were supplied to customers across the county (p. 108). Among the specialisms was that of the glass painters who designed and created what today are usually called stained-glass windows; historical records show that there was a concentration of glaziers in Stonegate, and excavations behind Stonegate, to the rear of 9 Blake Street, have uncovered a dump of about 5000 small pieces of glass, which must represent the debris from one of the glaziers' workshops.

Another workshop which seems to have focused some of its efforts on the ecclesiastical trade was a bronze-founder's premises excavated by YAT at the Bedern, just beside the College of Vicars Choral (p. 107) (**70**). The business had been started up in the mid to late thirteenth century and continued into the early sixteenth century. The workshop survived as the stone underpinnings for a series of timber-framed structures. It was identified partly by the number of hearths built from edge-set tiles, but principally by the remains of clay moulds which had been used in the casting process. Although only small fragments survived, their study has shown that

70 *Fourteenth- to fifteenth-century bronze foundry with central tiled furnace, bordered by an alleyway to left and top, at Bedern. Scale: 2m (6ft 6in).*

they were for making large circular castings, certainly including cauldrons but probably also including bells. Bell-founding was definitely practised in medieval York, as both historical records and the mid-fourteenth century bell-founders' window in York Minster show; the Bedern foundry demonstrates something of the reality of the working conditions and technical accomplishment of this industry.

Because, as we have seen (p. 43), the medieval city was an administrative centre for the county, for the northern archdiocese, occasionally for the English royal court and, for almost a century, for the Government of all northern England, there was much need for accommodation for all those involved. Before the Reformation, royalty could commandeer monastic quarters, often the Franciscan friary just outside the castle; later, domestic quarters in the former Benedictine abbey became the King's Manor where the Government of the North was based. For the most part, however, less exalted lodgings and premises were necessary; this kept a good number of unskilled and semi-skilled labourers busy, and also required the efforts of craftsmen including masons, carpenters, plasterers and tilers, glaziers, plumbers, pavers and labourers. Many were drawn to York because of the scale of its building programme and eventually established their own workshops, buying the privileges of being a Freeman of the City so as to be allowed to set up as independent contractors (**71**).

There were, of course, substantial and prestigious new or continuing projects which tempted and required experienced craftsmen – the Minster, which was under almost constant enlargement until 1472, guildhalls, the castle, or the city walls. Overall, however, the mainstay of the medieval construction industry was not in creating new buildings, but in repairing or renovating existing ones, both domestic and religious.

And for this they had to have access to raw materials, whether stone, timber, tiles and bricks etc. Some of these materials came from the immediate vicinity of York; the Vicars Choral, for example, owned tileworks at Clifton, only about 1km (1100yds) north-west of the city. Timber, or lead, however, came from rather farther afield, and was often bought from merchants rather than direct from producers. Timber was a very important resource, for until the mid-seventeenth century most secular buildings were timber-framed. From the twelfth century the tilers had already taken over several components of the builder's trade previously undertaken by others; firstly, thatched roofs had been replaced by the

longer-lasting tiles, and then, increasingly from the fourteenth century, panels of wattle and daub infill for timber-framed buildings had been replaced by 'wall-tiles', as bricks were known. Tiles were also used for hearths, for making chimneys, at least from the fifteenth century, and for flooring.

Stone, in contrast, could be freshly quarried for the most important and magnificent new buildings, using the traditional York sources for limestones in the Tadcaster and Malton areas, to the west and north-east of the city respectively; but there was also a significant amount of recycling going on. For example, over 400 pieces of reused stone were recognized during the excavation of the Vicars Choral College at the Bedern. They are shaped, moulded or decorated stones and can be identified through their form and quality as originating in various relatively early building campaigns at York Minster. When the Minster was further enlarged and embellished in new architectural and decorative styles they

71 *Seal of a stonemason reading, in partly abbreviated Latin (from just right of top)* S' THOME D' SWIN CEMEN-TARI, *which means 'the seal of Thomas of Swine, a stonemason'. Probably fourteenth-century. Height 28mm (1⅛in).*

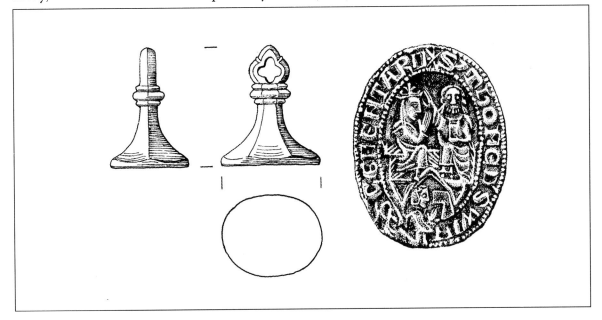

became redundant and were carried the 120m (375ft) across to the Vicars Choral, to be used as building rubble and incorporated into new structures there. (Thus it is possible to know as much, or more, about the former appearance of the Minster by studying stonework found elsewhere.) Any demolished stone structure could be converted into a cash asset by its owner, as long as there was a contemporary demand for new structures; and the ready availability of second-hand stonework resulted in some rather posh stones ending up hidden in unlikely places, like the group from some nearby church, perhaps St Peter the Less, which were reused to make an 8m (26ft) deep stone-lined well-shaft at Coppergate.

It wasn't only the building of houses which created a living for York residents; the renting of property was a lucrative source of income for those rich enough to invest. Lower down the economic scale the victualling industry – the supply of food and provisions for residents and visitors alike – was also a significant little earner for some folk, particularly women. Women were also recorded as often being small-time traders, but overall the references to them are relatively few, for they had no political rights and therefore did not appear in most official contemporary records.

Medieval York also drew residents and outsiders to its markets. The Horsefair is mentioned first in 1395; Swinelanding and Swinegate, mentioned respectively in 1300 and 1276, point to the existence of a pig market by the thireenth century; and the Thursday Market, in what is now called St Sampson's Square, is recorded by *c.* 1250, although what exactly changed hands there is not clear. The tradition of livestock markets, incidentally, was continued by the cattlemarket just outside the city walls, which held its last sales in 1970.

With so much commerce, so many people, so much coming and going, it is not surprising that other ways of making a living were practised in the medieval city. Several are commemorated in street names. What is now the decorous Nunnery Lane was, in 1241, *Baggergate*, a place perhaps where beggars badgered folk entering or leaving the city, or where badgers, hawkers or peddlers

tried to sell their wares. On the opposite side of town, by 1380, was *Herlothill*, identified as the modern St Maurice's Road, and taking its name from the Middle English for a rogue or vagabond. In 1301 an alley somewhere off Fossgate was know as *Trichour Lane* (Trickster's Lane), and from rather later (1576) there is the less ambiguous Thief Lane. A reference in 1329 to *Grapcunt Lane* (now Grape Lane) points to one location in the city where the oldest profession was practised, and prostitution in York was also decried in a sermon by the noted Franciscan friar Dr William Melton in 1426. Perhaps he had some of the Vicars Choral in mind (p. 110).

In addition to manufacturing, medieval York also functioned as a centre for regional, national and international trade. Indeed it was trade, rather than industry, which yielded great rewards for successful businesses. In *c.* 1125 there is a reference to ships from Ireland and Germany docking at York; in 1203–4 York was the seventh most important port in southern and eastern England, but the development of Hull in the thirteenth and fourteenth centuries initiated a decline in direct continental and other contacts – imported goods were offloaded at Hull and then carried up the Ouse to York. In the early fourteenth century, York's exports included grain to Gascony and grain and wool to the Low Countries, whence in return they imported cloth, wax, canvas and oats. By the later fourteenth century, when York was the richest provincial town in England, they were exporting wool and cloth, and importing wine from Gascony and the Rhineland, before transshipping some of it to places such as Berwick-on-Tweed. Other contemporary imports included Spanish iron, olive oil, wine, figs and raisins from Portugal, and herrings from Denmark and Scania. The Baltic trade in skins and furs was valuable for York merchants until they lost out to the German Hanseatic League in the late fifteenth cemtury; and Iceland was another trading partner providing fish in return for cloth and ale.

In the late fifteenth century York's overseas trade was in decline, as markets were closed to the

city, and it remained very much in the doldrums until the late sixteenth century when trade with the Baltic and even with Russia was resumed. In 1581 the merchants' guild was reorganized into The Society of Merchant Adventurers, and was granted a royal monopoly on all imports to York except for salt and fish. Their splendid Hall, first built in 1357, with its integral chapel and basement hospital/almshouse, is the most obvious symbol of their continuing existence (**72**, **73**, **74**)).

72 *Copper-alloy seal of the Mercers and Merchant Adventurers of York, showing the Holy Trinity between two ships, and the legend, in partly abbreviated Latin, SIGILLUM. COMMUNITATIS. MERCATOR'. S'. T'NITATIS. EOBORACI – 'the seal of the company of merchants of the Holy Trinity of York'. The Company paid three shillings (fifteen pence) for the seal in 1435. Diam.: 50mm (2in).*

73 *Merchant Adventurers' Hall, Fossgate, originally built 1357–61.*

The raw materials and foodstuffs that were imported are elusive in the archaeological record, and little enough has yet been seen of the medieval wharves where the ships berthed to discharge their goods. The same is true of the medieval ships themselves; so far, only a few fragments have been found.

The foreign contacts can, however, be recognized in foreign pottery vessels found at York. There are two main classes, tablewares and cooking vessels, which originate in two different sources. The cooking vessels are predominantly either frying pans or *grapen* (cooking pots with three feet and a handle, known in English as skillets or pipkins). They have a well-fired orange-red fabric, and were glazed internally with

a virtually colourless, good-quality lead glaze, which allowed them to be kept clean more easily. They were made in the Low Countries, and are mainly of fourteenth- to sixteenth-century date.

At the same time, jugs and mugs made at various kiln-centres in the Rhineland were also extensively imported to York. They were technically far superior to contemporary local (or even national) products, because they were fired to a much higher temperature (about 1200°C). This caused the clay to fuse and become more or less waterproof, tough and durable – hence they are commonly referred to as stonewares. Both types were brought to York by Dutch merchants and sold well (**75**).

While never a great manufacturing centre, York has been the home of some specialized industries, although the early ones were few and relatively small in scale. In the late seventeenth

74 *Merchant Adventurers' Hall, fourteenth century and later.*

75 *Two stoneware jugs and a Dutch cooking pot, representative of many found in York. Height of cooking pot: 0.21m (8¼in).*

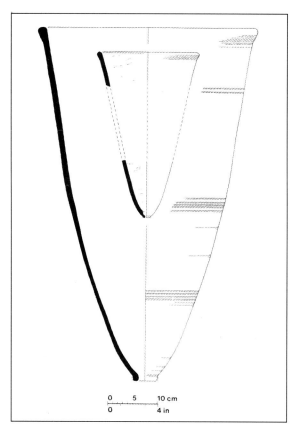

76 *Two late seventeenth-/early eighteenth-century ceramic moulds for making sugarloaves, from Skeldergate.*

century a sugar refinery was briefly in business near the waterfront in Skeldergate, where the partly processed imported sugar could be offloaded. The archaeological evidence for the industry is the distinctively shaped remains of pottery moulds for sugarloaves and jars for collecting syrup (**76**). Just downstream a glassworks had also opened. In the late eighteenth century an influx of Huguenots (French Protestants) brought skills in working tortoiseshell, ivory and horn to York with the Rougier family; they made fashionable combs, snuffboxes, card-cases and other items, and objects from their workshops have been found in excavations.

It was the second half of the nineteenth century which saw modern industry impinge on York. Flour milling has given the city one of its most pleasing industrial buildings (**colour plate 16**). The railway workshops were, until 1995, a major employer; more enduring has been the confectionery manufacture of Terrys, Cravens and Rowntrees (the latter now Nestlé). The most recent addition to the industrial base has been tourism which, in the late twentieth century, has been responsible for many changes to the city which may puzzle archaeologists a millennium hence.

6

Supernatural York

Religions represent a more or less continuous theme in the daily lives of York's people – beliefs in a superhuman controlling power or powers are evident in the archaeological record for most phases of the city's development. There are sometimes remains of buildings or structures which, by their peculiar shape, or decoration, can be interpreted as housing cults. There are artistic representations, icons and emblems which have a mystic rather than a practical purpose; there are also practical items which, in their shape or decoration, indicate that they also signify a spiritual dimension. There are overt proclamations of belief on inscriptions such as dedications or memorials; and there are mute testimonies in the form of burial rites (**77**).

Although only a tiny fraction of the evidence, particularly the cemetery evidence, has survived the disturbance of subsequent, and especially the most recent, centuries, there is still a relative glut of evidence for Roman religions and beliefs. In the first, second and early third centuries some of *Eboracum*'s inhabitants were cremated, and at Trentholme Drive debris from the coal-and-wood-fuelled cremation pyres was uncovered, revealing that objects including pottery, glass vessels and jewellery had accompanied the cremation. To the archaeologist's relief, because it is more informative about the individuals concerned, inhumation (burying the body intact) became the only standard rite from the third century. The graves were often furnished with grave goods of types similar to those from the cremations; a coin was

sometimes put into the corpse's mouth, perhaps to pay the ferryman to the otherworld; remains of animals, birds and oysters were quite commonly placed in graves, presumably as symbolic food for the after-life, while eggs may symbolize rebirth in an after-life. Sometimes shoes are the only articles for which there is evidence – their hobnails can survive although the leather rots (**78**).

The 35–41 Blossom Street cemetery reveals how Roman burial rites and customs varied (**79**). It was created in the early third century in an area previously used as a municipal rubbish dump, and was initiated by two burials inside a mausoleum. By *c.* 225–50 the original mausoleum was dismantled and rebuilt as a 6m- (19ft 6in) square structure (**80**), where more burials took place, one of which was accompanied by a pot which contained a complete chicken skeleton (compare p. 101). The relatively high numbers of gaming counters found in the mausoleum may not be fortuitous, but perhaps cast some light on ritual behaviour, giving a new insight into 'dicing with death'.

In the early fourth century the mausoleum was demolished, and some rubbish was dumped at the site before burial resumed again, with at least 25 inhumations recorded, and the likelihood that more had been destroyed by subsequent disturbance. Most of the new burials were aligned at 90 degrees to the earlier ones and, unlike Trentholme Drive, there was little intercutting of graves. Some individuals had certainly been buried in coffins, and a few were accompanied by

77 *Hypothetical reconstruction of a Roman burial in a vault at The Mount* (R.F. Raines; Reproduced by courtesy of the Yorkshire Museum).

an item of jewellery or some other offering. One third of the dead were aged under 20: male and female were equally represented.

There is no obvious clue to the philosophy or pattern of beliefs which inspired these various burial rites; fortunately, other types of evidence permit a closer approach to the gods. Most obviously there are inscriptions and dedications

offering thanks and honour to various deities. Some are well-known classical gods and goddesses – there are altars to Mars, Jupiter, Hercules and Fortune, and a relief carving of Mercury. Many of these gods, and other deities, appeared on the engraved gemstones of finger-rings, ensuring a close supernatural presence for the wearer (**colour plate 3**); other people pinned their hopes on good luck charms – phallic amulets were among the most popular (**81**). Among the favourite supernatural mentors, to judge by the number of references to them, were

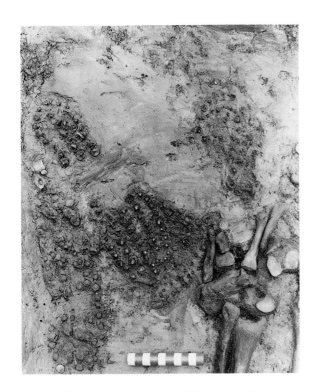

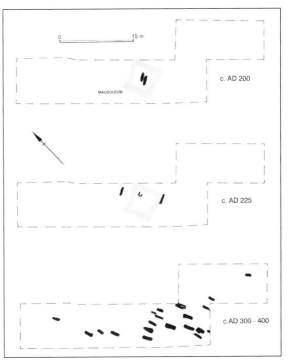

78 *Iron hobnails from two pairs of shoes survive by the feet of a late Roman burial at 16–22 Coppergate. Scale: 0.1m (4in).*

79 *The development through time of a Roman cemetery at Blossom Street.*

80 *Only foundation trenches survive to define a Roman mausoleum dated c. 225–50, at Blossom Street. Scale: 2m (6ft 6in).*

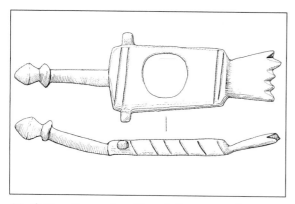

81 *Copper-alloy amulet with a phallus at one end and a gesturing hand at the other. Scale: 1:1.*

mother goddesses (a recurrent theme) and York's own *Genius*. Other dedicatees include *Britannia*, the emperor's divinity, Ocean and Tethys (p. 51) and Silvanus, the god of wild places and hunting. Some of the gods' names suggest by their form and their rarity that they were local or regional Celtic deities which had become part of the Romano-British pantheon; other names, such as the germanic Veteris, point to importation from abroad with military drafts.

Inscriptions such as that to the mother goddesses of Africa, Italy and Gaul (p. 52) seem to show their originators playing the supernatural field in a rather conventional and generalized way; but there are others which may testify to a more particular and individual faith. It may be more than a coincidence that a dedication to the Egyptian god Serapis was erected by the commanding officer of the Sixth Legion; the emperor Septimius Severus, who resided in York during the years 208–11, was a devotee of Serapis, and imperial devotion no doubt made it both fashionable and politically expedient to honour that god.

Another exotic cult almost certainly brought to *Eboracum* by the soldiery (for who else could it have been unless merchants?) was that of the Persian god Mithras. Mithraism became popular in the Western Empire, and several Mithraic sites are known in England, from the famous London temple, excavated by Sir Mortimer Wheeler in the early 1950s, to shrines on Hadrian's Wall. It was a mystery religion, only for men, into which

the devotee had to be initiated gradually in order to participate fully in the rituals and gain complete understanding of the battle between good and evil, light and darkness. The evidence for the cult at York takes the form of a dedication to Arimanius, the Mithraic god of evil, and a sculpture showing Mithras slaying the bull, with smaller figures below including an initiate receiving baptism into the cult (**82**).

Christianity was another Eastern mystery religion centred on the battle between good and evil which involved initiation into full participation. Again it was the military and the merchants who provided a mechanism for its introduction into *Britannia*, where it had arrived by AD 200. The dates when the first Christians reached *Eboracum*, or when the first Christian community was established, are unknown. Likewise there is no archaeological evidence yet for a Romano-Christian place of worship, either in a private house or in a communal church building. Yet there is documentary evidence that in 314, just three years after Galerius's Edict of Toleration had removed official state persecution, and a year after Emperors Constantine and Lucius recognized Christianity, Bishop Eborius of *Eboracum* attended the Church's Council of Arles, in southern France. He was one of only three British bishops who are recorded as attending (the others being from London and, probably, Lincoln); unfortunately there are no further records of the Roman bishopric.

Eboracum does, nevertheless, have its share of remains of Romano-British Christianity. The excavation at York Minster in 1967–73 unearthed a roof tile on which, before firing, the tiler had scratched the Greek letters *XP* (chi rho), the first two letters of Christ's name in the Greek alphabet (Greek being the original language of the Christian New Testament books). Such cryptic symbols, recognizable to the initiated, were current both when Christianity was a proscribed religion and after its acceptance by the Roman State. This particular piece may have signified pure *joie d'après-vivre*, or perhaps it was intended by its maker to ward off evil from the building.

Another Christian item comes from a grave found in 1901 at Sycamore Terrace, out along the northern Roman approach road to *Eboracum*. A woman's skeleton, lying in a stone coffin, was accompanied by several items of jewellery such as earrings, bracelets and beads, and an unusual Rhenish glass vessel, an assemblage datable to the mid-fourth century. What singles it out, however, is an openwork bone plaque, spelling out the Latin message SOROR AVE VIVAS IN DEO which translates as 'Sister, hail, may you live in God', a recognizably Christian sentiment. The plaque was probably attached to a casket which may have belonged to anyone, Christian or pagan, and the woman is not certainly a Christian; but the discovery is another strand of evidence for Roman York's Christian community.

It has sometimes been claimed that burials of Romano-British Christians can be recognized through a number of characteristics, including an east-west orientation and the absence of grave goods, that is, items for the use or adornment of

82 *Carving of scenes from Mithraic belief, found in Micklegate in 1747. Height 0.69m (2ft 3in)* (Reproduced by courtesy of the Yorkshire Museum).

the dead in the grave and in the next world. Now, however, these traits are recognized as having been widespread in the fourth century, and not just confined to the Christian community. The same is true of even more distinctive burial forms with supposedly Christian connotations. Some 40 plaster burials have been found at *Eboracum*; few places in Britain have more. In the (vain) hope, it is thought, of preserving the corpse, gypsum was poured around the shrouded body in its coffin. In fact the gypsum, although it retained a cast of the body and its shroud, also served to dry out the corpse.

The Christian idea of the dead being raised incorruptible at the end of the world can be seen as coinciding with the belief that plaster burials allowed long-term bodily preservation, and it may well be that among the plaster burials at York, and elsewhere, there are some which are indeed those of Christians. Yet the practice of plaster burial seems to have originated in North Africa before that area was Christianized, and to have spread within the Roman world, being adopted by wealthier sections of society, pagan and Christian, who could absorb the extra costs.

Whatever the numbers and doctrinal beliefs of *Eboracum*'s Christian community who, as just demonstrated, are archaeologically all but invisible at present, it is clear that non-Christian beliefs were deeply ingrained and continued to flourish. Representative of these are the discoveries made in the *colonia* in excavations at Wellington Row. During the third century, several pottery vessels were buried in the floors of the substantial rectangular stone building there, presumably as some sort of religious dedication. A little later a lamb was buried in a small pit close to one of the roof supports and later still, towards the end of the fourth century, when a dark-coloured silty loam was gradually accumulating within the derelict building, a pot containing a puppy was buried. All of these look like religious, or at least superstitious, activities.

Whether a Christian community focused on York continued to exist in the fifth century and later is not known. Christianity itself survived in the area, at least among the warrior leaders of British kingdoms such as Elmet, but the beliefs of any inhabitants of the city between the severance of political links with Rome and the arrival of the Anglo-Saxons are as elusive as the people themselves.

Although the Germanic gods and goddesses of the pagan Anglo-Saxons are superficially quite well known through the writings of Christian contemporaries, such works contain only a few pointers to their rituals and worship. Kingship and religion were closely related at this time, and it is therefore plausible that there would have been a temple in an Anglo-Saxon royal seat such as York. If there was, it hasn't yet been identified. Indeed the archaeological record nationally for Anglo-Saxon paganism is sparse, and this is certainly true of York, where burials provide the only tangible clues.

Best-known are the cremation cemeteries of the sixth century, found a short distance outside the walled town at The Mount and Heworth. The cremation urns are decorated, and often contain the burnt remains of various objects; research in the 1980s has identified the varying form and decoration of the pots, and the different artefacts within them, as indicators of social position rather than as having supernatural dimensions. This would accord with Bede's famous passage in his *Ecclesiastical History of the English People*, in which a Northumbrian pagan asserts 'we know nothing of this life, what went before and what follows', and might support the idea that objects buried with the dead were not put there to be useful in an after-life; if, that is, Bede's report was based on fact rather than *parti pris* poetic licence.

In what was basically a tribal society like the Anglo-Saxon kingdoms, acceptance of Christianity was a top-downwards process. In Deira, King Edwin came to conversion gradually, through a politically advantageous marriage to a Kentish princess who, following the papal mission to Kent in 597, was herself a Christian. The political alliance, sealed in the marriage, also brought to York a mission from Canterbury.

Edwin havered, but finally accepted the new religion after the safe birth of his first child, and following victory in battle over southern English rivals. The Christians' god had proved effective, and was presumably accepted quickly by loyalists in the royal entourage. Yet it may be questioned how quickly and thoroughly Christian beliefs were accepted by the rural population, other than among British Christians under Edwin's control.

Although Edwin built a wooden church in York where he was baptized in 627, its immediate rebuilding in stone which he began was unfinished when his defeat and death in 633 brought reverses to the new religion. The mission leader, Paulinus, fled York for Kent, and never returned, although his assistant, James the Deacon, remained. Edwin's immediate successors renounced Christianity in favour of old beliefs (the Christians' god was not so effective, after all) but after their defeat in turn the next Northumbrian king, Oswald, embraced 'Celtic' Christianity, which he had encountered when fostered in exile in Scotland. His success in battle reaffirmed Christian supremacy as the royal religion. There is no record of church-building in York for over 30 years, however; in the meantime the 'Celtic' bishops of Northumbria were based, if anywhere, at Lindisfarne, near the north Northumbrian royal seat at Bamburgh.

Only with the appointment of Wilfrid as Northumbrian Bishop in 664 was the bishopric's focus relocated at York. Wilfrid had to clean up Edwin's stone church; the account of this given in the *Life of St Wilfrid* suggests years of neglect. Whether or not this was the case, no archaeological evidence for these episodes has been discovered. Indeed there is no tangible trace of any of the various rebuildings of the pre-Norman cathedral church, nor of the monastery with its school which were established in the eighth century. The earliest Anglian Christian remains are, however, thought to be of about this date; they consist of fragments of gravemarkers, and were found in excavations at York Minster (**83**). These fragments represent only a dozen or so burials,

most probably those of churchmen; the graves and indeed the beliefs of the remainder of the city's population in the first century of Christian renewal are elusive.

It is possible, of course, that the Roman burial grounds beyond or on the edge of the city had continued in customary use in the fifth, sixth and into the seventh centuries. It would probably be very hard to substantiate this because so much of those Roman cemeteries has been destroyed or disturbed over the last few centuries. Identifying what might in any case be the rather unobtrusive graves of these dates, without gravemarkers, grave goods or eye-catching burial rites, would be difficult. Yet there are two places where possibly relevant evidence has been recorded. The first is at Castle Yard, a late Roman cemetery in which earlier coffins were reused. What makes this locale intriguing in terms of sixth-/seventh-century beliefs is the coincidence that various rather unusual items have been discovered hereabouts, including a bronze hanging bowl, and another bowl of a type identified as Coptic

83 *Late seventh- to early ninth-century fragmentary grave-marker from York Minster, with the name + LEOBDEIH. Width: 0.26m (10¼in).*

Egyptian. Unfortunately, they came to light in the nineteenth or very early twentieth century, and hardly anything is known about their archaeological context. Elsewhere, however, such things are often associated with burials, and so it is conceivable that they represent continuity in ritual use of this area at a time when eastern Mediterranean goods were available in Northumbria – when Christianity was a reason for such contacts. It is even possible that burials took place hereabouts because a new church, on or near the site of St Mary, Castlegate, had been founded as early as the seventh century. Unusual architectural fragments which might date to that time have been discovered there; a surrounding cemetery could then be explicable. The sceptic, however, will rightly point out that there is no firm evidence for either so early a church or any burials with bowls; further clues about the origins of the church and the fate of the Roman burial ground would be most welcome.

The second possible set of data for the rituals of the sixth–eighth centuries comes from Lamel Hill and its vicinity (p. 20). Below this mound was a cemetery in which corpses had been laid out on their backs with heads to the west and feet to the east. Children and adults, male and female, were represented, and the graves were carefully and apparently quite regularly spaced, 0.6–0.9m (2–3ft) apart. No objects had been buried with them, but remains of iron brackets and other fittings showed that at least some of them had been buried in wooden chests or coffins. The date of the cemetery is ambiguous – such burials are known from both the Roman and the Anglo-Saxon eras.

New evidence for burials hereabouts came in 1983, when excavations some 60m (200ft) east of Lamel Hill at Belle Vue House uncovered 38 skeletons. By the side of one were an iron knife and buckle datable to the Anglian period, and there was also a sherd of handmade Anglian pottery. However, the lid of a Roman stone sarcophagus may be an indication that the cemetery was initiated in the Roman period. The

burials, which were aligned approximately east-west, concentric to the summit of the hill, included at least nine in which the corpse had been mutilated or decapitated before burial. Sometimes the decapitated head was buried with the body, but in an unusual position such as over the knees. (**84**). One corpse had had its left foot removed, another both hands removed, and a third may have had two fingers cut off and placed between the thighs. Additionally, two of the decapitated corpses had been laid out with their feet to the west, the opposite of the norm.

Explanations for this seemingly bizarre collection of mutilations are made difficult by the uncertainty over their date; the Roman coffin lid reminds us that decapitated burials and mutilations were an occasional Roman custom as well as an Anglo-Saxon one. The rites, particularly decapitation, could be interpreted as sacrifices, as executions, as attempts to lay the ghost of the dead, or as a rite of veneration for the head as the seat of wisdom or the spirit. In the pre-Roman period some Celts practised head-cults; perhaps this persisted, or perhaps this was a parallel Germanic cult which the Anglo-Saxons maintained. Whatever the motive for what now seem gruesome rituals, they could be contemporary with the early Northumbrian Church of the seventh–eighth centuries, and may demonstrate

84 *An Anglian burial at Belle Vue House, near Lamel Hill, with the skull laid at the knees.*

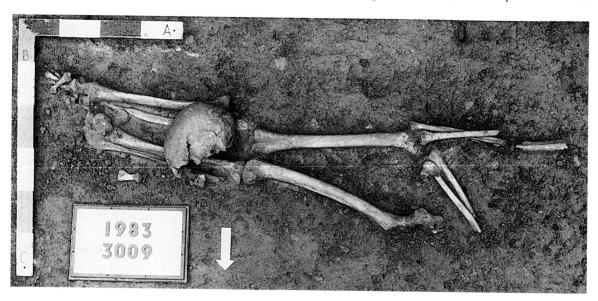

the wide range of beliefs that were current at a time generally thought of as the 'Golden Age' of Northumbrian Christianity.

Contemporary writers say that the 'Golden Age' left its mark in stone buildings, glass windows and sumptuous fittings made by metalworkers, textile-makers and others. The closest we can come to this is through some middle-ranking metalwork (**colour plate 4**) and some high-quality (and some mediocre) stone carving. A good example is a piece found in the York Minster excavations, decorated with a vinescroll plant design inhabited by a variety of animals and birds (see **68**). This ornament was native to the Mediterranean, and was introduced along with Christianity itself; the production of such works became as integral a part of the life of York's cathedral/monastic community as did the scholarship for which the city was famous in the eighth century. A Norman writer reports that a large block of the Roman fortress had been owned by the Church since 685, and if suggestions that the monastic church dedicated to Holy Wisdom was in the former Roman *colonia* are correct, then an even more widespread area of the former city was in ecclesiastical hands. Despite this, however, there is no firm evidence for any other churches in *Eoforwic*.

As might be anticipated, the religious beliefs of Viking Age York offer some continuity and some contrasts with *Eoforwic*. Once again a group of non-Christian immigrants, attempting to control a potentially hostile kingdom, encountered Christianity. Within 20 years the Scandinavians, who had already shown a pragmatic approach in their appointment of Christian Anglian puppet kings, supported the coronation of a Christian convert of their own. They thereby appeased some Anglian sensibilities by superficially removing one of the differences between them, and further assured themselves of the support of Archbishop Wulfhere (c. 854–c. 900) who seems to have been prepared to be flexible in his political allegiance. Although the religious affiliations of most subsequent Scandinavian kings aren't known, the assumption is that most were nominal

Christians, or at least not anti-Christian; only Olaf Guthfrithsson (939–41) seems to have had the political stance of an out-and-out old fashioned Viking.

Contemporary writings illuminate aspects of the beliefs of the Anglo-Scandinavian population at large, although they are insufficient to allow an assessment of how these beliefs may have changed as the generations passed. It is particularly tantalizing that there is no substantial written clue to beliefs during the late ninth–mid tenth centuries, the period of Scandinavian domination. From *c.* 1000 however, there is the *Law of the Northumbrian Priests* which indicates that all sorts of non-Christian behaviour was still prevalent in Northumbria at this date; this, however, may owe as much to a limited acceptance of Christian belief by the pre-Viking Anglian country folk as to Scandinavian heathendom.

In archaeological counterpoint there are several strands of evidence. Perhaps the most direct, as well as one of the earliest, is a series of four burials uncovered by Peter Wenham in the churchyard of St Mary Bishophill Junior Church. Among them was one skeleton with a silver armlet and a smaller silver ring interjoined on one arm, and a second skeleton associated with a knife, a sharpening stone, a buckle plate, and a silver penny of a type minted in York *c.*905–15. Although these are not richly furnished burials, they nonetheless stand out from the contemporary norm (at least insofar as we currently recognize it). Both their date, as indicated by the coin, and the presence of grave goods, particularly the silver jewellery, suggest that these are the graves either of Scandinavian settlers or of their descendants. The burials mingle the Christian custom of churchyard burial with the Scandinavian rite of interment with grave goods, and could be interpreted as striving for a mutually acceptable middle ground. Alternatively, one can chose to emphasize the customary aspects of one or other side of the religious divide, and argue for pagans making use of a convenient burial plot, or Christians simply not dogmatically concerned about the incidental furnishing of the grave with a few personal items.

Taking the acculturation line, however, which emphasizes the move towards a hybrid culture with, for some people at least, a hybridized attitude to religion, there are other archaeological pointers in this direction. For example, the coin found in the Bishophill burial is what is called a St Peter's penny, because it has on it the words 'St Peter's money', which presumably reflect the cathedral's dedication to St Peter. On some of the St Peter pennies, however, that religious motto shared its place with the representation of a sword and the hammer symbol of the Norse god Thor (**85**). A more overt and official mingling of religious symbols is hard to imagine.

Something of the same attitude can be discerned in the decorated gravestones of Anglo-Scandinavian date which have been found at many of the city's churches. A particularly telling series comes from York Minster, where one gravemarker depicts episodes from the Germanic legend of Sigurd the dragon-slayer (**86**). It is suggested that such scenes are heroic rather than pagan, and compatible with the

85 *Head of an iron coin die dated 921–6/7 from 16–22 Coppergate, incised in reverse with the abbreviated legend 'St Peter's money', but with a Viking sword and Thor's hammer symbol. Diam.: 28mm (11/8in).*

86 *Side of tenth-century grave-slab from York Minster. The hero Sigurd kills the dragon Fafnir. Length: 1.3m (51in).*

notion of Christ as a hero; even so, this is surely a reflection of the Scandinavian component of Anglo-Scandinavian culture and belief.

Just as there is a proliferation of carved grave-stones in the Anglo-Scandinavian period when, in another sign of changing times, stonecarvers now worked for a secular clientele as well as church-men, so too there is evidence that many churches were founded at this time (**87**). Often it is the carved stonework itself which suggests that the church where it was discovered was in existence in the Viking Age, but in a random handful of cases excavation has shown that the church was first erected in this period. These churches are always small structures, either a simple rectangle or of a basic nave-and-chancel form. They were clearly designed for small congregations, and it is most likely that they were built by the more important and prosperous inhabitants as their own personal places of worship. Other considera-tions – having a personal priest to pray for the founder, his or her family and prosperity; prepar-ing a suitable setting for eventual burial; impressing other townsfolk; making money out of church dues – may have played a part in any individual case, but we shall never know. Thus, however, York's parochial system was developed from what may have been the previous monop-oly of the cathedral.

Soon after the Norman conquest of York, a new Norman archbishop, Thomas of Bayeux, was installed and the Viking Age cathedral church was totally replaced. What mattered as much to William as to Thomas was that the new building was in the Norman Romanesque style, one which would impress and overawe as both a setting for worship and as a statement of Norman supremacy. Like the Norman castles, the cathe-dral was an overbearing symbol of the new order. Not much survives from this church except its foundations, but they are a technical triumph, a belt and braces job to gladden the heart of the most pessimistic engineer. They also testify to the enormous quantity of oak that was available to make the timber grille which under-pinned the entire structure (**26, 27**).

87 *Eleventh-century dedication stone of St Mary, Castlegate. Height 52.5cm (20½in).*

From the time of William I the rich endowed other new religious buildings in York. Two monasteries for Benedictine monks, a Benedictine nunnery and a Gilbertine monastery (**88**) had been founded by 1202, as well as St Leonard's Hospital (**89**). Lower down the ecclesiastical scale, other parishes seem to have been founded at this time. In the thirteenth century a new wave of fri-ars reached York, along with other continental and English towns; Dominicans, Franciscans, Carmelites, Augustinians and, although only briefly, Friars of the Sack, all had friaries in the city, courtesy of generous royal and aristocratic endowments. There were also other institutions, such as the College of Vicars Choral of York Minster at the Bedern, where the 36 priests who sang the services in the Minster lived a communal life; or the College of St William, built *c.* 1465, which housed 23 priests whose main responsibili-ties were to conduct memorial services for their patrons at altars in the Minster.

Other options for the pious included the enlargement or beautification of existing churches (**colour plate 9**), the founding of chantry chapels where prayers were said for the souls of donors and their families, or the building of hospitals. Religious and charitable feelings could also be given tangible expression in the fraternities or guilds.

For founders and donors, it was kudos, piety and after-life insurance. For some of the religious themselves there was clearly a yearning

88 *The Gilbertine monastery at Fishergate. Wall trenches and foundations of the church are to the left, the nave much cut above by graves. To the right of an unexcavated strip is the cloister garth (at top), with a limekiln at its centre; around the cloister are other monastic buildings, rubbish pits etc. The two parallel curving ditches and small post-holes nearby are from the Anglian occupation c. 700–850.*

89 *St Leonard's Hospital, Museum Street; part of the infirmary built 1225–50.*

for spiritual values and the imitation of Christ. The magnificent ruins of the Cistercian Fountains Abbey are testimony to the soul-searching that took place in St Mary's Benedictine Abbey in York in 1132 when a group of monks challenged what they saw as their abbey's overworldly attitudes and decamped to Skeldale, near Ripon. Almost four centuries later, in 1537, the Prior of York's Dominican Friary, John Pickering, paid the ultimate penalty for his beliefs; he was executed for his role in the Pilgrimage of Grace, the popular uprising which supported traditional religion.

Other priests who do not figure in the historical records presumably fulfilled their vows faithfully and diligently, but archaeology has combined with documentary studies to show that the Vicars Choral priests were less than wholly reverent. Their original thirteenth-century communal dormitory arrangements were subdivided into private bedrooms and later still, as their numbers decreased and more space became available, they occupied individual houses. The luxury of privacy was just as well, given the propensity exhibited by some of them to invite prostitutes into the Bedern. Study of the vicars' diet and their personal belongings has also shown that their lives were more luxurious than had previously been suggested (**colour plates 7 and 8**). Their tableware, for example, included the sorts of glass vessels usually associated with palaces and castles rather than monastic sites; and a large number of coins, tokens and gaming pieces which had been lost beneath the floorboards of the College Chapel hint at inattention to divine service. One coin from Bedern is a *dinero* of James II of Aragon (1291–1327), and may represent another aspect of medieval religious life, a pilgrimage to the famous shrine of St James at Santiago de Compostela, in north-west Spain.

Archaeology has also demonstrated York's role as a centre of pilgrimage, to the shrine of St William, an archbishop who died in 1154. Although arguably an unlikely candidate for sanctity, his cause was vigorously promoted by the cathedral's canons, doubtless with one eye on the popular cult of St Thomas Becket at rival Canterbury. In 1223 he was proclaimed a saint, and thereafter his tomb and shrine in the Minster attracted pilgrims. Both monuments were destroyed in the mid-sixteenth century at the Reformation, but fortunately their appearance can be reconstructed because parts of them were dismantled and buried in the Minster precinct, where they were found in the eighteenth century (**90**). St William was also depicted in a great early fifteenth-century window in the Minster choir, which includes a scene of a devotee giving thanks at the shrine by presenting a wax model of a miraculously cured leg. The normal paraphernalia of pilgrimage was available at the shrine – souvenirs in the form of lead-alloy containers of holy oil or water, decorated with appropriate imagery reflecting the saint, were available, and these have been found in excavations at Coppergate, York – the only ones yet recognized (**91**).

A cult which achieved even greater prominence at York Minster in the fifteenth century was that of another Archbishop of York. Richard Scrope was executed in 1405 at Clementhorpe, just south-east of the city, for his part in a popular insurrection against centralized power. Within months his tomb in York Minster was attracting pilgrims and was the scene of alleged miracles. He was commemorated in the Minster's glass, but despite efforts of laity and clergy alike he was never canonized. Nonetheless, in just one year, 1419, £150 was offered at his tomb, and this reverence helped to pay for rebuilding the Minster's central tower. Veneration continued until the Reformation. Archaeological evidence for the popularity and devotion to the cult was found in the aftermath of the fire which gutted York Minster in 1829. Nearly 100 silver pennies and half-pennies were recovered from the area of the

90 *Reconstruction of the principal shrine of St William in the choir of York Minster, behind the high altar screen. The protective wooden canopy above the silver-gilt reliquary is shown raised* (John Hutchinson; Reproduced by courtesy of the Yorkshire Museum).

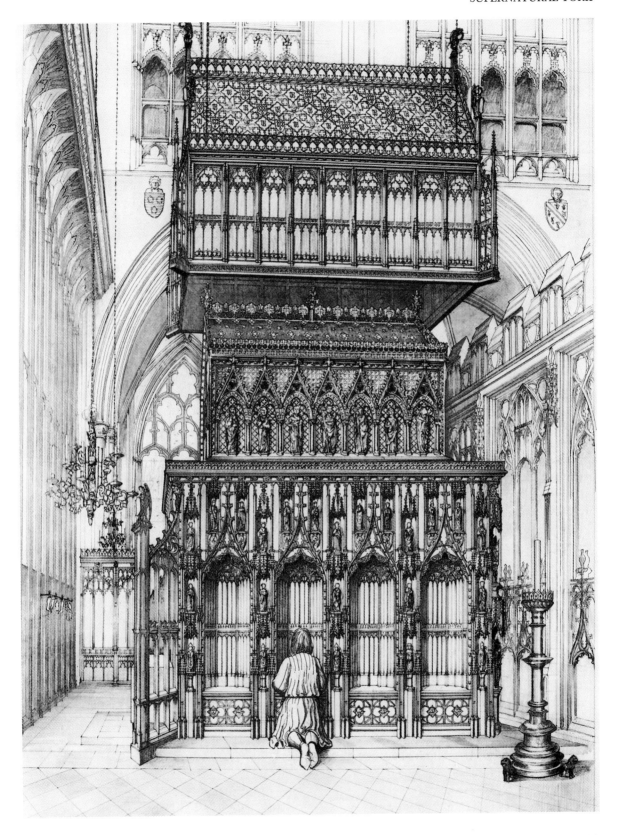

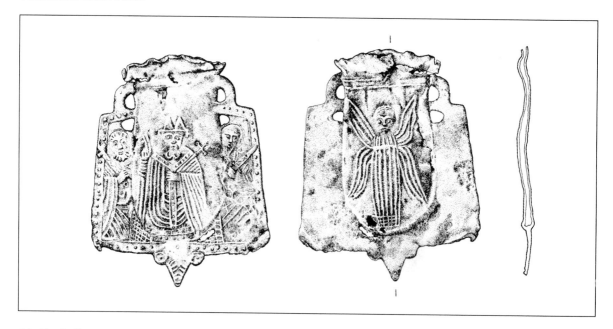

91 *Lead-alloy* ampulla, *a container for holy oil or water, from 16–22 Coppergate. Front: an archbishop (?St William of York) flanked by Saints Peter and Paul; rear: an angel. Scale: 1:1.*

tomb, the latest being of Henry VII (1485–1509). Among them were three Anglo-Gallic, one Venetian and three Scottish coins – not necessarily testimony to foreign pilgrims, but an index to the small change circulating in fifteenth-century York.

As for previous periods, one of the most obvious places to gather evidence for religious beliefs is in the cemeteries of medieval York. These reflect much more than just a degree of care for Christian based tradition. At the very top end of the social/ecclesiastical scale, the burials of two thirteenth-century Archbishops of York, the most important medieval churchmen in northern England, were examined in 1968 and 1969 during restoration works in the Minster's south transept. Both archbishops lay in stone coffins, lead-lined in one case, with a painted lid in the other (**colour plate 6**), and one lay beneath a splendid and ornate stone effigy and monument. Both had been buried in appropriate ecclesiastical garb, the head resting on a cushion which in one case had been embroidered. With both bodies

was a badge of office, a gold episcopal ring with a large central sapphire and small surrounding jewels, rubies and emeralds in one case, garnets and emeralds in the other. Each had a pastoral staff, another indication of rank, and also a chalice and paten, tools of the priestly trade (**92**).

These two high-status burials stand out sharply from the hundreds of other medieval interments recovered from forgotten York churchyards. There, only a few gravemarkers or monuments have been found, and these were merely upright plain stone slabs. Almost the only graves which contain objects buried with the corpses are those of priests, which have a chalice and paten of lead-alloy. Otherwise people were placed in the grave without emblem or adornment; even personal jewellery is a rarity, although finger-rings are occasionally found, and there is an instance of a child aged eight–ten with a necklet of twisted wire. Yet, exceptions could be made. Two individuals at All Saints, Peasholme, which was demolished in the sixteenth century, were buried with a papal bull, in one case clasped in the skeleton's left hand, in the other apparently placed near the head. The bull was a special and recognizable type of lead seal which was attached to papal documents as a means of authentication. Bulls, if well enough

93 *Lead papal* bulla *(seal) of Pope Urban III (1185–7) found in a grave at All Saints, Peasholme. Diam.: 37mm (1½in).*

92 *Archbishop Godfrey de Ludham (died 1265) buried with a cushion, mitre, pallium, chalice, paten, pastoral staff and ring.*

preserved, can usually be dated because they bear the name of the issuing pope – in these two instances Pope Urban III (1185–7) and one of the many Popes Clement. We'll never know precisely what these particular documents were

about; were they a form of status symbol or some form of passport to the after-life (93)?

Occasionally there is evidence that attempts had been made to preserve the body; Archbishop de Ludham, for example, had been embalmed. In a few other burials, mainly of the eleventh–thirteenth centuries, the corpse was laid on, or covered to some extent with, charcoal. This may have been an attempt to soak up bodily liquids and thus somehow enhance preservation; alternatively, it may represent a ritual with a significance now lost. A wide variety of medieval grave types has also been discovered, presumably in part a reflection on the status of the deceased's family. Apart from simple, earth-dug graves, there are graves with mortar linings, with a mortared base lined with ashlar blocks to make a simple composite stone coffin, with rough slab or stone linings, linings of unused ceramic roof tiles, and, at the top of the range, monolithic stone coffins.

Some individuals were buried in a shroud; the textile decays, but bronze pins and antler tines probably served as shroud fasteners. A rector of St Helen-on-the-Walls forbade any covering for

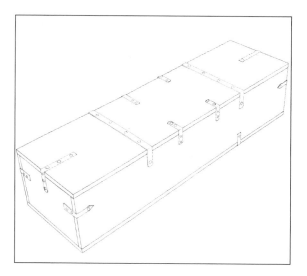

94 *Reconstruction of an iron-bound wooden coffin from the Jewbury cemetery.*

his body other than a shroud, but it is clear that shrouded corpses were sometimes put into coffins. Usually only rusty nails survive, but moist soil conditions in Swinegate allowed the preservation of a rare series of twelfth–thirteenth-century coffins from the redundant churchyard of St Benet's. These coffins are mainly held together with wooden dowels or joints, rather than with nails – a reminder to the archaeologist that lack of nails in a grave doesn't necessarily mean that the deceased was laid to rest uncoffinned. In the cemetery at Jewbury it was discovered that, contrary to current practice, medieval Jews were frequently buried in coffins held together with iron nails and even, in some cases, with quite elaborate iron fittings (**94**).

One aspect of burial practice did appear to single out medieval Jews from their Christian contemporaries. While the Jewbury burial ground was carefully and regularly laid out in rows, with few instances of intercutting graves (**95**), most of

95 *The regularity of grave-cuts in the Jewbury cemetery.*

the Christian churchyards were comprehensively disturbed by later graves dug through earlier interments. Skeletons or corpses were often unceremoniously dismembered, and the bones shovelled to one side. Sometimes they were simply left where they had been displaced, sometimes they were gathered together in groups and reinterred in charnel pits. Excavation near the long-demolished St Wilfrid's Church, between Lendal and Blake Street, suggests that charnel was sometimes reburied in squarish wooden boxes or containers.

It was force of circumstances which necessitated the Christian grave-diggers' cavalier treatment of previous generations – the urban graveyards were limited in size and simply could not accommodate the dead century after century, and overcrowding was the reason why the parish graveyards were eventually closed in 1854 when the situation was even worse. York's Jewish community had been able to buy a plot of open land outside the city walls, and had then bought an adjacent plot in order to extend their cemetery. Pressure of space was by no means so acute as for the inner-city parishes.

There is, however, evidence that fourteenth-century landowners might have no qualms about erasing traces of religious use. St Benet's Church in Swinegate was united with the nearby St Sampson's in 1263, having been used for perhaps only 200–300 years. Contemporary reports tell that in 1316 coffins (*sarcophoga mortuorum*) were visible on the site; by 1338 it was 'covered with rubbish'. Archaeology has demonstrated that the cemetery was covered over by a cobbled surface and a variety of mundane secular activities then took place. The dead were soon forgotten. This may also have been the case in the several instances where the edges of graveyards at a street frontage were developed with houses in order to make money for the church in question. There are good surviving examples at Holy Trinity, Goodramgate, where Lady Row was erected in 1316, and also on the Patrick Pool side of St Sampson's and on Micklegate outside Holy Trinity. It's not certain, however, whether or not these buildings were erected over burials.

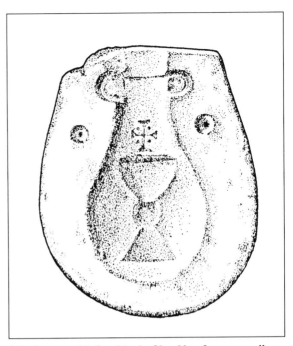

96 *Stone mould, found in the Shambles, for an* ampulla, *a container for holy oil or water. The symbols of the cross and chalice represent the body and blood of Christ, especially venerated on Corpus Christi Day. Height: 72mm (2 ¾ in).*

Another part of the spectrum of medieval religious observance was the annual performance of the Corpus Christi miracle plays, today commonly called the 'mystery plays'. From 1325 York was gripped with celebrating the Feast of Corpus Christi (**96**), an observance which involved processions. One of these was organized by the Corpus Christi Guild, which included many of the city's craftsmen. Eventually it incorporated a series of dramatic presentations, one by each guild or group of guilds, presenting a pageant or episode from the biblical story which was somehow related to their profession; the texts of 47 plays still survive. They were performed on wagons in a vast processional production which started at Toft Green, alias Pageant Green, just inside Micklegate Bar, and went down Micklegate, across the Ouse, along Coney Street, up Stonegate, turned right into Petergate and Colliergate and ended up outside All Saints Church in Pavement. The performance, which must have lasted from dawn until midnight, was noted for its merriment, feasting and drunkenness; as well as its religious *raison d'être*, it was an opportunity for fun. It was suppressed at the Reformation.

A fifteenth-century view of the perils of religious damnation, and a means to avoid them, are both shown in the painted glass of All Saints, North Street. The Fifteen Last Days of the World represents the horrors to be confronted (**colour plate 10**); the Corporal Acts of Mercy shows a good man behaving charitably. Exhortation and trepidation were powerful preaching partners.

There were, however, other facets to later medieval belief and custom which are less often recognized. In a late fifteenth-century bronze foundry at Bedern (p. 89) a pit had been dug just inside the door, and the remains of a cat and several hens placed in it. This recalls earlier dedicatory offerings, for example from the Roman period (p. 101), and although it may be no more than a superstitious habit, it represents a distinct strand in contemporary belief. And from the rather different milieu of the Vicars Choral College, next door to the foundry, came a group of early fourteenth-century pottery and glass fragments of types associated either with industry or with alchemy; another possible guide to the broad spectrum of late medieval beliefs.

How most of the city's population felt about the Reformation isn't known, but the generation which spanned the mid-sixteenth century certainly witnessed great changes which resulted from it. The monasteries, friaries, nunnery and hospitals were shut, the lands sold and most of the buildings pulled down. Substantial structures, with much magnificent architecture, disappeared from the city's skyline; some of their stone was burnt in the limekilns which are often found on the former ecclesiastical sites (see **36**).

Some ecclesiastical sites were adapted for new purposes. In 1253 the Carmelites had founded their first priory in the Horsefair, now Union Terrace, but by the end of the century they had moved to a better site within the walls, near Fossgate. Their original priory was transformed

into St Mary's Hospital to accommodate a master, two assistant chaplains and six aged and infirm chaplains. After the Dissolution the site was used in 1557 for the refoundation of the grammar school of St Peter, which had previously been situated in St Mary's Abbey; the school remained there until Civil War damage forced it out (**97**).

In time, with the diversity of dissenting Protestant sects, a new series of buildings was to arise to house the worship of Methodists, Unitarians, Presbyterians, Quakers and others. Perhaps the finest of these is the Unitarian Church in St Saviourgate, originally built for the Presbyterians in 1692 (**98**). The densest concentration was erected in Priory Street in the later nineteenth century; ironically this area, sometimes called York's 'Holy Land', lies over the remains of one of the Benedictine priories and, arguably, of the Anglo-Saxon monastery. Another group, including the Methodist and Salem Chapels, stood in Saviourgate/Spen Lane. Roman Catholicism was also resurgent; the Bar Convent, just outside Micklegate Bar, had been a boarding school since 1686, and St Wilfrid's Church, impinging on the prospect of York Minster in Duncombe Place, was but the successor in 1864 to earlier chapels in this vicinity.

The graveyards of what had become, at the Reformation, Church of England parish churches, held all the city's dead until the Quakers (1667), Presbyterians (1793) and Congregationalists (1816) opened burial-grounds. When a cholera epidemic swept England in 1832, a new site just outside the city walls, close

97 *Four main stages in the development of a medieval building at the Horsefair; hatched lines are new walls at each phase.*
1 ?The nave and chancel church of the Carmelite Friary, late twelfth–thirteenth century.
2 St Mary's Hospital, infirmary hall (left) and chapel (right), fourteenth–mid-fifteenth century.
3 St Mary's Hospital in a developed, quadrangular form, mid-fifteenth–mid-sixteenth century
4 St Peter's School, mid-sixteenth–mid-seventeenth century

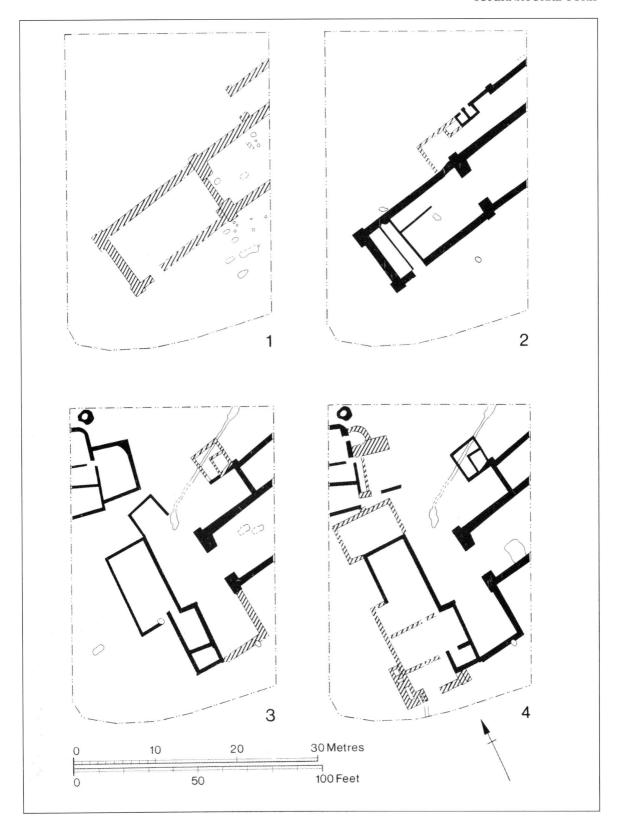

98 *The classic simplicity of St Saviourgate Presbyterian Church (now Unitarian), built in 1692.*

to the more recent railway station, was consecrated so that bodies could be buried sufficiently deeply to avoid remaining a health hazard, and many of the 185 York victims were buried there. In 1837 a new, public cemetery was opened just to the south-east of the city, where there can be found fine individual monuments as well as mass graves of the Victorian poor.

The beliefs of York's late twentieth-century residents and visitors appear to echo the diversity of the Roman period, and one intriguing aspect is the interest (albeit often superficial) in the supposed ghosts which allegedly haunt York. Two of the most freqently mentioned stories, regardless of their archaeological inconsistencies, are a troop of Roman soldiers, and a Jewess seeking sanctuary

from the mob in 1190. If you are sceptical of such ghost tales, but would like to be in touch with the past, take comfort; as I hope this book has shown, the fact is that ancient York and its people do survive, albeit often anonymously (**99**), transmitted to the present and into the future through the remarkable archaeological remains buried below the modern city.

99 *Anonymous, probably fourteenth-century, copper-alloy seal from Bedern. A squirrel surrounded by an inscription in Middle English* (starting top right) *I CRAKE NOTIS – 'I crack nuts'.*

Visiting York

York is a walker's city, to be viewed from the city walls (open dawn to dusk daily) and penetrated on foot. Two complementary maps – *'Roman and Anglian York'* and *'Viking and Medieval York'* – published by the Ordnance Survey/RCHM/York Archaeological Trust, place archaeological discoveries in relation to the modern street plan.

The Association of Voluntary Guides to the City of York offer free informative walking tours of the historic centre every day at 10.15a.m., starting at Exhibition Square; from April to October there are also tours at 2.15p.m., and an evening tour at 7.00p.m. during June, July and August. Tours with special themes can be arranged on request. For details, contact the Honorary Secretary, Association of Voluntary Guides, De Grey Rooms, Exhibition Square, York Y01 2HB or telephone 640780 between 9.30a.m. and 11.30a.m. (Monday to Friday only).

The Yorkshire Museum* in Museum Gardens, between the remains of St Mary's Abbey and the Roman fortress walls, includes much archaeological material from York; a fine cross-section of the objects recovered by collectors and antiquarians, as well as those from more recent excavations, is usually on display. For information, telephone 629745.

The Jorvik Viking Centre*, in Coppergate Walk, includes a simulation of the Viking Age tenements excavated there by York Archaeological Trust, as well as the preserved remains of the tenth-century buildings and a selection of the artefacts found in and around them. For information

and bookings telephone 613711.

The Archaeological Resource Centre*, housed in the redundant St Saviour's Church in St Saviourgate, shows through its 'hands-on' collections how archaeologists use the objects they find to recreate the past. For information and bookings telephone 613711.

In 'The Foundations'*, below York Minster, Roman and medieval remains found during the excavations of 1967–73 are displayed; the Crypt contains mainly Norman works. For information on opening times, telephone 624426 or 639347. The 'World of the Minster', in St William's College, off the east end of the Minster, provides a valuable introduction to the cathedral, its history, fabric and people. For information contact 637134. The Minster is open daily; the Foundations and the Crypt have slightly more restricted opening times.

The York Story*, in the redundant Church of St Mary, Castlegate, provides a very useful introduction to the buildings and people of medieval and later York, with models, dioramas and graphics. For information telephone 628632; for bookings telephone 633932.

The Merchant Adventurers' Hall*, entered off Fossgate and Piccadilly, gives a marvellous insight into a top grade medieval guildhall. For information and bookings telephone 654818.

York City Art Gallery, in Exhibition Square, houses a fine selection of artists' views of York spanning several hundred years; some are usually on display. For information, telephone 551861.

Clifford's Tower*, the keep of York Castle, is open daily (closed at lunch time during winter). For information telephone 646940.

Fairfax House*, in Castlegate, is one of the finest eighteenth-century town houses in England, and is filled with a famous collection of contemporary furniture. For information telephone 655543.

York Castle Museum* contains a wealth of pre- dominantly eighteenth- to twentieth-century material, including a recreation of a Victorian Street. For information telephone 653611.

* Admission charge
** The telephone dialling code for York is 01904

Further reading

Archaeology

The Archaeology of York, a continuing series, ed. P.V. Addyman, published by the Council for British Archaeology in 20 chronological, topographical and thematic volumes, contains the results of YAT excavations, and other complementary data and discussion.

D. Phillips, *Excavations at York Minster* I and II (HMSO 1995 and 1985 respectively) report the Roman–Viking Age and the Norman cathedral respectively.

L.P. Wenham, *Excavations at Trentholme Drive* (HMSO, 1968) is the definitive account of a Roman cemetery.

P.J. Ottaway, *Roman York* (Batsford/English Heritage, 1993) and R.A. Hall *Viking Age York* (Batsford/English Heritage, 1994) are companions to this volume.

S. Jennings, *Medieval Pottery in the Yorkshire Museum* (York, 1992) is a well-illustrated introductory guide.

For the development of antiquarianism and archaeology, see P.V. Addyman, 'Archaeology in York 1831–1981' in C.H. Feinstein (ed.), *York 1831–1981*, (York, 1981), pp. 53–87

Buildings

The Royal Commission on Historical Monuments of England has published five volumes of its Inventory of Monuments in York: *Eboracum/Roman York*, *The Defences, South-West of the Ouse, North- East of the Ouse*, and *The Central Areas. York. Historic Buildings in the Central Area* is a shorter, mainly photographic version of the latter.

J. Hutchinson & D.M. Palliser, *Bartholomew City Guides – York* (1980) contains a useful historical introduction, and is the best modern commentary on the city's buildings; Eric Gee, *The Architecture of York* (York, 1979) is more selective. D.Buttery, *The Vanished Buildings of York* (York, c. 1990) and H. Murray, S. Riddick & R. Green, *York through the Eyes of the Artist* (York, 1990), are both well-illustrated reminders of what was once there, while R. Davies, *Walks Through the City of York* (1880), is an unillustrated but fascinating account of the city from a mid-Victorian perspective.

History

The Victoria County History – the City of York, ed. P. Tillott (Oxford, 1961) and A. Stacpoole (ed.), *The Noble City of York* (York, 1972) are the major, detailed modern historical surveys.

D.M. Palliser & M. Palliser, *York As They Saw It* (York, 1979) is a nice collection of comments on York spanning over a millennium.

Index